SUPPORT AND STRIKE!

A CONCISE HISTORY OF THE
U.S. 9th AIR FORCE IN EUROPE

by John F. Hamlin

First published 1991 by
GMS Enterprises,
67 Pyhill,
Bretton,
Peterborough,
PE3 8QQ

ISBN 1 870384 10 5

Typeset by G. A. Graphics, Bury St Edmunds

Cover painting by Charles J. Thompson GAvA, AFAA

Produced by the author

Printed by Cambridge Printing Services Ltd.

Maintenance being carried out to the port engine of a B-26 at Boreham
[via Bryan Jones]

CONTENTS

An unusual picture of three of the 9th Air Force's aircraft types in formation: P-47 [A8:X] of the 366th FG; P-38 [9D:G] of the 370th FG; and F-6 [VX:U] of the 69th TRG
[IWM neg. EA24276]

INTRODUCTION

Few World War Two organisations responsible for such a profound effect on the successful outcome of the conflict have received such sparse recognition as the United States Ninth Air Force. Compared with its sister force, the Eighth, which was, admittedly, in action in the United Kingdom for a much longer period than the Ninth, little has been published in Great Britain about the 'Cinderella' force's activities.

This book is an attempt to record, in concise form, possibly as a starting point from which other books may evolve, the history of the Ninth Air Force in the European Theatre of Operations, from October 1943 through its move to the Continent from June 1944 to its eventual inactivation in December 1945. To redress another wrong, the non-flying Commands, usually neglected, are also included as far as space permits, but only a series of books of several thousand pages would allow all the multitude of ground units to be mentioned. IX Air Force Service Command and IX Air Force Engineer Command are of particular interest, and it is hoped that comprehensive accounts of their activities will be written at some future date.

The author wishes to offer sincere thanks to the following individuals who contributed information to this book.

Dave Benfield, whose considerable knowledge of the Troop Carrier Groups was invaluable.
Aldon Ferguson, Hon. Sec. of the Burtonwood Association.
David Hall, for his specialist knowledge of glider operations.
Bryan Jones, who has studied the activities of the 394th BG in detail.
Bob Mynn, Chairman of the Buddies of The Ninth Association.
Dave Osborne
Norman Roberson.
Bruce Stait, for information on the 397th BG.
Ken Wakefield, author of 'The Fighting Grasshoppers', for his knowledge of the independent liaison squadrons.
And many others. Those who provided photographs are of course acknowledged individually.

The Buddies of The Ninth Association exists to perpetuate the achievements of the men and aircraft of the US 9th Air Force in Europe and to maintain friendly relationships with veterans and their dependents as well as to carry out research into 9th Air Force history. Membership is open to interested people on both sides of the Atlantic, and details are available from:

Victor J. Lewis,
52 Spring Lane,
Fordham Heath,
Colchester,
Essex, CO3 5TG,
England.

ABBREVIATIONS

(A)	Austria
AA	Anti-aircraft
AAA	(a) Allied Airborne Army; (b) Anti-aircraft Artillery
AADA	Advanced Air Depot Area
AD	(a) Air Depot; (b) Airborne Division
ADC	Air Defence Command
ADG	Air Depot Group
AF	Air Force
AFSC	Air Force Service Command
ALG	Advanced Landing Ground
ARC	Aircraft Replacement Centre
ASC	Air Support Command
ATG	Air Transport Group
ATS	Air Transport Squadron
ATW	Air Transport Wing
(B)	Belgium
BAD	Base Air Depot
BADA	Base Air Depot Area
BC	Bomber Command
BD	Bombardment Division
BG	Bombardment Group
Brig. Gen.	Brigadier General
BS	Bombardment Squadron
BW	Bombardment Wing
CADA	Continental Air Depot Area
Capt.	Captain
Casevac	Casualty evacuation
CBW	Combat Bombardment Wing
C-in-C	Commander-in-Chief
CO	Commanding Officer
Col.	Colonel
D-Day	Allied invasion of Europe, 6.6.44
DF	Direction Finder
DUC	Distinguished Unit Commendation
DZ	Dropping Zone
EAB	Engineer Aviation Battalion
EAR	Engineer Aviation Regiment
EC	Engineer Command
ELS	Emergency Landing Strip
ETO	European Theatre of Operations
(F)	France
FA	Field Artillery
FB	Fighter Bomber
FC	Fighter Command
FG	Fighter Group
FW	Fighter Wing

(G)	Germany
(H)	Holland
HQ	Headquarters
IDG	Intransit Depot Group
IDS	Intransit Depot Squadron
(L)	Luxembourg
Lt.	Lieutenant
Lt. Col.	Lieutenant Colonel
LS	Liaison Squadron
LST	Landing Ship Tank
M	Medium
Maj.	Major
Maj. Gen.	Major General
MP	Military Police
MR&RS	Mobile Repair & Reclamation Squadron
MTO	Mediterranean Theatre of Operations
NFS	Night Fighter Squadron
N/K	Not known
OG	Observation Group
OS	Observation Squadron
PG	Photographic Group
PoW	Prisoner of War
PRG	Photographic Reconnaissance Group
Prov.	Provisional
PRS	Photographic Reconnaissance Squadron
PSP	Perforated Steel Planking
QM	Quartermaster
RAF	Royal Air Force
RCD	Replacement Control Depot
R&R	Refuelling and Re-arming
SC	Service Command
SG	Service Group
TAC	Tactical Air Command
TAD	Tactical Air Depot
TAF	Tactical Air Force
TCC	Troop Carrier Command
TCG	Troop Carrier Group
TCS	Troop Carrier Squadron
TRG	Tactical Reconnaissance Group
TRS	Tactical Reconnaissance Squadron
UK	United Kingdom of Great Britain and Northern Ireland
USA	United States of America
USAFE	United States Air Forces in Europe
USSTAF	United States Strategic Tactical Air Force
VE-Day	Victory in Europe Day, 8.5.45

CHAPTER 1: The U.S. 9th AIR FORCE

Before the entry of the United States of America into the Second World War on 7 December 1941, a body known as V Air Support Command had been constituted. In April 1942 this new Command was redesignated as the U.S. Ninth Air Force and as such was sent to Egypt in the autumn of that year. The Ninth's Groups began operations in November 1942 in support of the Allied drive across Egypt and Libya and took part in the fighting in Tunisia and the invasions of Sicily and mainland Italy.

When the initial planning for an invasion of continental Europe began, it was realised that an essential constituent of the scheme would be a tactical air force. To provide this element, the 9th Air Force was effectively disbanded in the Middle East and was re-formed on 16 October 1943 at a Headquarters at Bushey Hall, Watford, just north-west of London. The 9th's new missions in life were clearly defined: to take a major part in the war of attrition leading up to the invasion and to follow the invasion forces on a fully mobile basis toward the eventual conquest of Nazi Germany.

To achieve these ends, the 9th Air Force was set three priorities

    One: to gain and hold air superiority

    Two: to disrupt enemy lines of communication

    Three: to destroy enemy forces at the front line in close cooperation with ground troops

Attacks on enemy installations and production facilities behind the lines were not to be part of the 9th Air Force's task — such missions would continue to be left to the Royal Air Force and the 8th Air Force's heavy bombers. To meet all the requirements, a very rapid build-up of aircraft and men was envisaged.

Upon the re-formation of the 9th Air Force, four existing medium Bombardment Groups, all operating B-26s, were transferred from the 8th Air Force's VIII Air Support Command, and shortly became the 98th and 99th Bombardment Wings of IX Bomber Command, the only Command of the 9th Air Force which was already fully operational.

Early in its new existence the 9th Air Force adopted procedures designed to give its Groups maximum mobility and operational flexibility. From the first, operations carried out by the four Groups from their English bases included a number of diversionary raids on airfields near the coast of France to help the 8th Air Force and to begin the 'softening-up' process leading up to D-Day. Fighter support in the shape of three Fighter Groups began to arrive in November 1943 and by 8 December they had been placed under the control of 70th Fighter Wing, itself part of IX Fighter Command, commanded by Brig. Gen. Quesada. Two of these Groups, the 357th at Raydon and the 362nd at Wormingford, flew P-47s, while the 354th FG at Box-

P-38J 268071 was the first 9th Air Force fighter aircraft to land in France after the Allied invasion; note the shipping in the near background.
[IWM neg. EA27168]

These 373rd FG pilots seem to be paying close attention at a mission briefing taking place at Woodchurch ALG. Lt. Col. M. J. Ingelido, 373rd FG Ops. Officer points to details of a mission on 21 July 1944 for 36 aircraft to escort medium bombers to a raid on Le Mans [via Alan Wright]

ted used P-51s. By Christmas 1943 the latter were routinely accompanying 8th Air Force 'heavies' to targets deep inside Germany. Also part of IX Fighter Command was the 67th Reconnaissance Group, which flew vital missions in support of the Bombardment Groups, using Spitfires, F-6s, P-51s and A-20s operating from Membury, Middle Wallop, Greenham Common and Keevil, all in central southern England.

IX Air Support Command was activated on 4 December 1943 at Aldermaston Court in Berkshire, and on re-designation to IX Tactical Air Command on 4 April 1944, took control of four Fighter Wings, the 70th, 71st, 84th and 100th, from IX Fighter Command. Just after D-Day, IX TAC headquarters was moved to France, and by the end of June 1944 five of its fighter-bomber Groups were fully operational there. Mobility was achieved by creating a 'superadvanced' headquarters to move with that of the First Army, with which IX TAC operated closely.

A further tactical Command, XIX Air Support Command, was activated on 4 January 1944, and took control of the 100th and 303rd Fighter Wings, being redesignated as XIX TAC on 4 April 1944. It became operational on the Continent, in co-operation with the Third Army, in August 1944, having taken over some of IX TAC's Fighter Groups.

To carry the huge masses of men and equipment which would be needed on and from D-day, IX Troop Carrier Command was formed, under the command of Brig. Gen. Williams. By early December 1943 IX TCC comprised three Troop Carrier Groups, all under the control of the 50th Troop Carrier Wing, all three Groups using the ubiquitous C-47 and C-53 aircraft.

Early in 1944 IX BC learned that it would receive four more B-26 Groups which were in an advanced stage of training in the United States, plus three A-20 Groups. The first of the new B-26 Groups for 98th and 99th BWs arrived late in January and the last in April, by which time there were over 700 B-26s on Essex airfields. Meanwhile, the three A-20-equipped Groups had arrived by sea to form 97th BW. Rapid expansion of IX ASC/TAC also continued, resulting in five Groups of P-47s, one of P-38s and two of P-51s being in place by the end of February 1944, under the control of 70th and 71st Fighter Wings. In addition, 10th PRG was transferred from the 8th Air Force to operate from some of the same bases that the 67th TRG used, and flew F-5s. IX TCC also continued to expand rapidly, with five TCGs in being or in the course of formation by the end of February 1944.

IX Air Force Service Command had come fully into being by February 1944, and controlled six Tactical Air Depots, at North Witham, Stansted, Grove, Kingston Bagpuize, Chilbolton and Membury, tasked with the supply of aircraft and spares to all 9th AF units as required. Use was also made of the enormous 1 Base Air Depot at Burtonwood, alongside the 8th Air Force, whose responsibility 1 BAD was.

With the invasion of Europe planned for the summer of 1944, it became clear that 9th Air Force, in order to take full advantage of opportunities which presented themselves, often had to mount operations much more rapidly and flexibly than any other US Air Force. Parameters were now defined under which the 9th Air Force would operate following D-Day (Operation Overlord).

1. A rapid move to the Continent would be made very soon after the successful launch of Overlord.
2. At first, 9th Air Force units on the Continent would be serviced from the UK, but before long rear supply positions would come into use.
3. The 9th Air Force would provide total air defence behind the US 1st (later 12th) Army front line.
4. IX Engineer Command would construct or repair all the airfields required by the 9th Air Force.
5. All tactical and service units of the 9th Air Force would have to be as mobile as the Army.
6. A system of highly sensitive control of airborne tactical units would be vital in order to provide precise coordination with the armies on the ground. For this requirement there was no precedent.

During the Spring of 1944, most of the Fighter Groups left their Quonset-hutted bases for the Advanced Landing Grounds of southern England, where only tented accommodation was available, to be closer to the south coast and thus to enemy-held France. Operating conditions at the ALGs could also be made to approximate to those on the planned temporary airstrips in Normandy. The eleven Fighter Groups controlled by IX TAC were now located on airstrips mainly in the Hampshire area, some of them airfields of a more permanent nature, while the XIX TAC's seven Groups were all at ALGs in Kent or Sussex. The 67th TRG and the 10th PRG stayed put to continue their operations, while two night-fighter squadrons arrived in England without their P-61 aircraft, later moving north for training.

IX BC continued to keep up the pressure during April 1944, the targets including V.1 sites in the Pas de Calais, railway marshalling yards and important bridges. Air Chief Marshal Air Trafford Leigh-Mallory, RAF, remarked at the time that the 9th Air Force was by far the most effective force in knocking out these types of target. From the beginning of May the 9th despatched more than a thousand aircraft each day, weather permitting, against targets in Normandy and the Pas de Calais, but giving no clues on where the invasion would take place. Priorities One and Two, set for the 9th the previous October, had now been accomplished.

As D-day neared, IX BC, IX TAC and XIX TAC were given the responsibility of destroying all major road and rail bridges in northern France, while 10th PRG was tasked with carrying out very low-level reconnaissance sorties along the beaches of the whole of the French Channel coast. Meanwhile IX TCC Groups arranged and carried out Exercise Eagle, a huge 'dummy run' for the Command's participation in Overlord, and IX EC, which had been busy on the construction of some of the ALGs in southern England, amassed vast quantities of PSP for airstrips and thousands of items of mechanical equipment.

D-Day, 6 June 1944, when it eventually arrived, demanded an even greater intensity of 9th Air Force activity. The success of the concentrated 'softening-up' process soon became obvious, as the Luftwaffe was unable to oppose the cross-channel armadas of landing-craft and other vessels to any great effect. Even Reichsmarshall Hermann Goering admitted that the Allies' successful invasion was very largely due to the activities of the several Allied air arms, including, of course, the 9th Air Force. The main contributions made by the 9th were the prevention of rapid movement of German forces, thus allowing the Allies to secure firm positions, and overwhelming mastery of the air, enabling Allied ground forces to move forward with much more freedom.

As the opening blow of 9th Air Force participation in Operation Overlord, IX TCC C-47s dropped thousands of paratroopers in the Cherbourg peninsula, while IX BC B-26s and A-20s were airborne before dawn to attack gun batteries on what was to be known as Utah Beach. Later that day, the bombers switched to attacks on communication centres, supply depots and other vital targets behind enemy lines. The fighter-bombers of IX TAC and XIX TAC flew about 2300 sorties in twenty hours to cover cross-Channel shipping, protecting the beach-heads, destroying any bridges left standing, and at last, providing co-operation to the ground forces under the long-established Priority Three. Subsequently, former Wehrmacht commanders confirmed that the incessant fighter-bomber attacks on roads and railways succeeded in preventing the movement of troops and supplies to the beaches. The commanders felt that, had they been able to move their reserve forces forward, the outcome might have been quite different.

The 67th TRG and 10th PRG were kept intensely busy during the first few days of Overlord, but in general reconnaissance was not well catered for in the original 9th Air Force plans. It was later felt that each TAC should have had the use of at least one TRG, with another TRG for the use of Air Force HQ.

IX Engineer Command units landed on Utah Beach on D-Day and at 21.15 hours completed an emergency airstrip just behind the beach. Further IX EC units came ashore on Omaha Beach the following day and an airstrip suitable for C-47s was in use by noon on D-Day + 3. By D-Day + 5 four batallions of aviation engineers were ashore and were building three airstrips for fighter-bomber Groups, five of which had moved from their ALGs in England to Normandy by D-Day + 16. From their new airstrips these Groups made an all-out attack on the defences of Cherbourg on 22 June. Nine all-weather airfields were in use in Normandy by D-Day + 24, and another seven were being constructed, testimony to the tremendous effort and pre-planning put in by men of IX EC.

July 1944 saw the movement of IX BC's 98th BW Groups, the 323rd, 387th, 394th and 397th BGs, from their Essex bases to airfields along the Hampshire coast; the 97th and 99th BWs stayed put for the time being. By 24 July four airfields for light and medium Bomber Groups and one for a Reconnaissance Group were under construction and eighteen Fighter and Reconnaissance Groups were operating from fifteen airstrips in Normandy. In September the three A-20 equipped BGs of the 97th CBW and the four BGs of the 99th CBW with B-26s, all crossed the Water to be based on these new airfields, leaving several English bases strangely quiet.

Air defence responsibility was provided from shortly after D-Day by IX ADC, which comprised two provisional air defence Wings and two RAF Sectors, each equipped with night fighters and fighter control facilities. Control of AA guns became a severe problem due to being under ground force command, and was complicated by the huge number of Allied aircraft airborne at any time. After two months or so, IX ADC was given command of all AA positions behind the army's rear flank.

25 July 1944 saw the carrying-out of Operation Cobra, the

Air Vice Marshal Sir Trafford Leigh-Mallory, RAF, on a visit to the 394th BG at Boreham, stops to chat to a ground crewman   [via Bryan Jones]

Little-known code 3A is displayed on a C-47 of the 53rd TCS, 61st TCG, seen here with an interested group of men watching C-47s fly overhead

most effective sustained close-support operation yet mounted. The object was to saturate an area of about 2½ square kilometres south of the main St. Lo to Periers road where a concentration of German troops was located, and the operation succeeded in completely disorganising the enemy, allowing a breakthrough by Allied troops over the totally cratered terrain. Co-operation between air and ground forces was excellent, and set a precedent for all combined operations.

XIX TAC became operational in France on 1 August 1944 and went into action with the US Third Army to begin the Allied "end-run" across France. This Command was given extensive responsibilities over a wide geographic area stretching from Brest to Paris and beyond. Simultaneously, XIX TAC fighter-bombers took part in the siege of Brest, gave cover to armoured columns advancing rapidly toward Paris, and were entrusted by Gen. Patton to protect the Third Army's right flank along the river Loire.

Determined German forces attempting to create a wedge between First and Third Armies in the Avranches area were effectively prevented from doing so by the IX TAC Groups. IX TAC proved that supremacy in the air was fully effective in denying the enemy any chance of exploiting success on the ground. Both IX and XIX TACs, with assistance from RAF Typhoons, attacked every target requested by US ground forces, successfully disrupting powerful armoured columns and totally nullifying the mobility of the German counter-attacking forces. The same three organisations combined again in mid-August to strike against enemy troops retreating from the Falaise gap, turning that event into a disorderly rout.

The rapid German withdrawal, faster in fact than had been anticipated or hoped for, put the mobility of IX EC, IX AFSC and IX ADC under severe stress. As a result, the forward movement of these Commands depended on day-to-day availability of road transport. IX AFSC, for example, was obliged to move its units and supplies over ever-lengthening and altering lines of communication, while IX EC was kept at maximum stretch carrying out its task of building temporary airstrips for the operational Groups. Considerable hindrance was felt by IX EC at this time due to difficulties in moving the huge volumes of construction supplies forward. Little help was provided by other organisations whose job it was to provide transportation when and where needed.

Late in August 1944, four Groups of the 98th Bombardment Wing moved from their English bases to France, creating the

desired effect of extending the circle of available targets and allowing the Groups to make use of better weather conditions on the Continent.

When in late August/early September Allied forces approached the Siegfried Line, enemy resistance hardened, and the offensive turned into a more static one. This situation lasted until December, when the Germans mounted a major counter-attack in the Ardennes forest area of Belgium. Meanwhile, still carrying out air operations, although reduced in number by bad weather, 9th Air Force moved its operational Groups to positions as close as possible to the front line in order to take advantage of shorter routes and longer dwell times. The airfield availability situation had now greatly eased, due to the capture of many ex-Luftwaffe airfields in the Paris area. IX EC was able to repair these for use not only by C-47s of the England-based TCGs carrying vital supplies and by Fighter Groups, but by the other seven Bombardmant Groups, which moved over from England during September and October 1944. This strategy had not been included in the invasion planning, but was made possible by priorities given to the movement of fuel, bombs and ammunition by rail for IX BC use. It was realised that continued effort in destroying enemy targets behind the lines was vital, and no trouble would be spared in making this happen.

The period of static warfare and poor weather allowed a breathing space as far as operations were concerned, but the opportunity was taken of replenishing stocks of bombs and ammunition, some types of which were now in short supply. Transport was an ever-present problem, and it is to the credit of IX AFSC, whose men worked shifts twenty-four hours a day, seven days a week, that the system did not break down.

During September and October 1944, 9th Air Force moved its Headquarters from England to France and reorganised its administrative and operational procedures in readiness for the final assault on Germany via the Siegfried Line. The 'directorate' system was adopted, with one senior officer responible for operations at Advanced HQ and another officer looking after administration at Main HQ, both answering to Maj. Gen. Hoyt S. Vandenburg, the 9th AF's Commanding General. At much the same time, the 9th AF's commitments increased when the US Ninth Army moved into position. It was the 9th Air Force's responsibility to provide a TAC to work with each Army, and the XXIX TAC (Prov.) was therefore constituted, becoming operational on 2 October 1944. Components of XXIX TAC came from IX FC, which by then had virtually disbanded, IX

TAC and XIX TAC.

The 9th Air Force's only two squadrons of P-61 night fighters, which had moved from England to France in July and August 1944 to carry out defensive operations, were assigned to IX and XIX TACs in October to carry out a more aggressive role. Very good results were achieved and it was then realised that an even better showing could have been made had more squadrons of this type been available.

Meanwhile, IX ADC's sphere of influence continued to grow as the Allied armies pressed on eastwards. It remained the task of this Command to defend the port installations at the Normandy beach-heads, and everything from there to important areas just to the rear of the front line. In addition, great success was shown in defending Belgian cities against the V.1 flying bombs which were now being launched against them. The port of Antwerp in particular was targetted by these weapons, but such was the effectiveness of IX ADC's efforts that only a very small number of the several thousand V.1s making for Antwerp got through, the great majority succumbing to the Command's AAA batteries.

One of the largest airborne operations of the War was mounted in September 1944 at Arnhem in Holland, a name now synonymous with enormous effort and little success. The operation was something of an unknown quantity from the start, as information on any defences in the area was sparse. 9th Air Force's Commander, however, believed firmly that that the TACs could quickly knock out any AA gun positions which might cause trouble, and the Supreme Commander gave the order to proceed. General Brereton was proved correct in his belief, very few 9th AF aircraft being lost to flak or to enemy fighters. The 9th AF's Fighter Groups were afterwards highly commended for their part in the Arnhem operation in knocking out such flak positions as there were.

By now, 9th Air Force Groups were being vectored ever closer to the front line. Two thirds of all sorties were at the request of those in the front line area, and 9th Air Force fighter-bomber strikes were very effective in wiping out artillery, supply trains, armoured columns and ammunition dumps on the enemy side of the ever-moving line. When the front became more static, however, Allied artillery units were able to catch up and the need for close cooperation between the 9th Air Force Groups and the ground forces decreased a little. Priority Two missions — preventing a German build-up — then became the norm, the Group leaders checking first that no Priority Three tasks — disruption of the enemy at the front line — were required before attending to Priority Two. The planning required for almost all such operations was carried out by the TACs rather than by 9th Air Force HQ, which only formulated the main, long-term, strategy.

Giving photographic coverage of the battle area during the advance across France and beyond, the 9th's few PR Groups worked unceasingly. A Directorate of Photography and Reconnaissance was established in 9th Air Force HQ in September 1944, but facilities for processing and printing the photographs were always inadequate, forcing 9th Air Force to rely to a large extent on the better equipment of the 8th Air Force.

Notwithstanding the tremendous effort put into their task by the 9th Air Force's three TACs, the enemy managed to build up some strength by December 1944 with a view to relieving the growing Allied pressure on the Siegfried Line. On 16 December von Runstedt began a counter-offensive in an attempt to isolate Allied forces east of Liege, Brussels and Antwerp. On von Runstedt's side was a period of very bad weather which had prevented the operation of 9th Air Force reconnaissance aircraft and a shortage of Allied troops in the area, coupled with an element of surprise. To make the most of his chance, von Runstedt put far more Luftwaffe aircraft into the air than usual. Nearly 150 of them were destroyed, however, in the first two days of the campaign, when, for fighters, the weather was just suitable for flying and the 9th Air Force's TACs were able to get airborne. Then the weather really closed in, preventing almost all daytime operations, but the nights were clearer and this above all

Lighter moments for men of the 397th BG at Rivenhall

[B. Stait]

Air Vice Marshal Sir Trafford Leigh-Mallory addressing 434th TCG enlisted men at Aldermaston while on a whistle-stop tour before D-Day. Note the L-5, 298992, and the Oxford, possibly AM484, and the three 'gas-guzzlers'
[D. Benfield]

emphasised the already-known fact that there was a severe lack of night instrusion facilities in the 9th Air Force.

Aircraft on hand and operational when the counter-offensive began comprised 669 P-47s, 126 P-38s, 486 B-26s and 87 A-20s. P-51s are not mentioned in the official listing. During the second half of December losses caused by battle and other incidents were 98 P-47s, 30 P-38s, 68 B-26s and 19 A-20s. Replacement aircraft were needed urgently, particularly P-38s, which had been in short supply since D-Day.

During the counter-attack, centred on the forest of Ardennes, the 9th Air Force was for the first and last time on the defensive. The advanced HQ was at Luxembourg, but telephone lines to IX TAC and XXIX TAC were cut, and these Commands were then transferred, temporarily, to the control of the British 2nd Tactical Air Force, the air partner of the British 21st Army Group, which took control of the US 1st and 9th Armies. Three Fighter Groups were transferred to XIX TAC from the other TACs and two 8th Air Force Fighter Groups, the 352nd and 361st, redeployed from their English bases for a short time under 9th Air Force control to assist. Furthermore, in order to eliminate this threat once and for all, the complete B-24 equipped 2nd Bombardment Division of the 8th Air Force was put under the control of the 9th Air Force for a time.

The weather cleared two days before Christmas, and for five days — no holiday for anyone that year — the 9th Air Force was able to make the most of the opportunity. Putting all its power behind the effort, 9th BD launched a campaign of destruction of roads and railways, forcing the enemy back because he was unable to sustain the movement of supplies and reinforcements to his Ardennes front line. Following up after the BGs had done their work, the TACs' fighter-bombers put the finishing touches by hunting and destroying all enemy vehicular traffic, until on 28 December the weather worsened again. At Bastogne, troops of the 101st Airborne Division, under siege, were helped by 9th Air Force TACs, which attacked targets which the Armies were unable to deal with due to a shortage of ammunition. The two night-fighter squadrons also played their part, but once again the lack of night intruder aircraft was painfully evident.

On New Year's Day 1945 the Luftwaffe put everything it had, about 600 aircraft, into attacking Allied airfields, but lost over half the force in the process, owing to the effective handling of the situation by IX ADC and the three TACs. Although a number of 9th Air Force airfields were raided and some aircraft destroyed, replacements were quickly on hand and operations

were not unduly affected. One well-organised mission carried out by the bombers of 9th BD on 22 January consisted of an attack on a bridge over the river Our. The bridge was eliminated, causing a huge traffic jam, which the 9th Air Force TACs then proceeded to destroy, nearly 3000 vehicles being put out of action. By the end of January 1945 the Ardennes counter-offensive was over, and Allied forces were advancing once more.

Resuming their drive towards the river Rhine, the US First Army, with which IX TAC operated, and Third Army, supported by XIX TAC, met little real resistance. Meanwhile a campaign of attacks on important communications centres around the Ruhr valley began, carried out mainly by 9th BD Groups with support from the TACs in mopping up vehicular traffic. On 22 February all available aircraft, both 9th Air Force and RAF, took part in Operation Clarion, with the intention of bringing to a halt the entire railway network in west Germany. This was one of the 9th Air Force's most rewarding days in the ETO, and afterwards the railways in the target area were of little use to anyone.

Ten days later, the US First Army reached the river Rhine and crossed the famous 'Bridge Too Far' at Remagen to create a bridgehead on the east side. Intense opposition by the Luftwaffe, which put up Ju87s and Me262 jet fighters, and by Wehrmacht artillery, was felt, and TAC elements of the 9th Air Force set up air patrols over the area. Other TAC Groups went ahead in a campaign of destruction of German airfields, and the 9th BD medium bomber force took part by bombing the few railway installations still operating which could support any flow of German troops and supplies toward the bridgehead.

The US Third Army made the second crossing of the Rhine on 22 March 1945 and was supported in the same way by 9th Air Force TAC Groups. The Third Army's line then advanced at a rapid pace toward central Germany, Austria and Czechoslovakia, meeting decreasing opposition on the way. In the north, however, where the Canadian First, British Second and US Ninth Armies were advancing, a third Rhine crossing was required. This one, destined to be the last airborne trooping operation of the Second World War, was carried out by two Divisions of the First Allied Airborne Army, which dropped in the Wesel area on 23 March. In this totally successful operation, IX TCC hauled troop-carrying gliders from airfields in France, meeting little or no opposition in the air. The TACs flew fighter-bomber sorties to eliminate any dangerous flak positions, and not a single IX TCC aircraft was lost to enemy action.

From this point on, the war was virtually over, and as far as

This chequered jeep was equipped with VHF radio for use as a runway control vehicle at Matching [via R. Mynn]

Twenty-wheel articulated aviation fuel bowser is one example of the many types of motor vehicle used by the 9th Air Force [R. Mynn]

9th Air Force was concerned was a time of mopping-up, the TACs destroying as many enemy aircraft on the ground as possible, a severe fuel shortage having restricted Luftwaffe operations. IX and XXIX TACs flew only defensive and reconnaissance missions from the end of April, but XIX TAC continued to support the US Third Army in its drive southward toward Bavaria. Some Groups from the other two TACs were transferred to assist XIX TAC in this final mopping-up task.

Early in May 1945 the 9th Air Force flew its final offensive missions and all its constituent units began preparing for de-activation or redeployment. Some Groups and their supporting units were destined for rapid transfer to the United States, where they would, if necessary, re-equip for further service in the Pacific zone, while others, probably more slowly, set about the task of disposal of equipment and posting of personnel before disbandment. IX AFSC, however, became deeply involved in the huge task of disarmament which had begun in the autumn of 1944 when German bases in France had been recaptured. To this end, vast depots were set up under IX AFSC control, and for several months the programme of collecting

equipment for scrapping or for reparations continued.

Gradually the component Groups and other units of the 9th Air Force in Europe departed, and on 2 December 1945, almost seven months after the end of hostilities, 9th Air Force was de-activated, any remaining units being transferred to the control of other authorities which would administer the post-war American forces of occupation. So ended the brief but incredibly active life of a force without which the outcome of the Second World War would undeniably have been quite different. During its 18 months of combat service in the ETO, the 9th Air Force flew 368 500 sorties; 2 944 aircraft were lost and 3 439 men were killed or were listed as Missing In Action. 4 186 enemy aircraft were destroyed in the air and 365 on the ground and 2 768 were damaged. The 9th grew from four to forty-five combat Groups, from less than 300 to over 1 100 bomber aircraft, from nil to over 3 000 troop-carrying aircraft and gliders and from a tiny nucleus to over 200 000 personnel. As a barometer of activity, the following table gives the numbers of aircraft on charge for each month between November 1943 and May 1945.

1943		
November	523	
December	670	
1944		
January	940	
February	2269	
March	3631	
April	4558	
May	5026	
June	4802	
July	4402	Some TCGs detached to MTO
August	4752	
September	3290	Transfer of IX TCC to 1st AAA
October	3436	
November	3558	
December	3445	Transfer of some FGs to 1st TAF
1945		
January	3508	
February	3695	
March	3867	
April	4055	
May	4633	Transfer of some FGs from 1st TAF

Commanding Officers:	Lt. Gen. Lewis H. Brereton	(12.11.42)	
	Lt. Gen. Hoyt S. Vandenburg	8. 8.44	
	Maj. Gen. Otto P. Weyland	23. 5.45	
	Maj. Gen. William E. Kepner	4. 8.45	— 2.12.45

436th TCG C-47s and CG-4s lined up at Melun/Villaroche on 24 March 1945 for action in the Rhine crossing operation
[Lawrence Riordan]

A-20s of the 671st BS, 416th BG taxy out at Wethersfield   [Merle Olmsted]

13

CHAPTER 2: THE COMMANDS

IX BOMBER COMMAND

IX Bomber Command, which had seen service in the Middle East, transferred to the United Kingdom with 9th Air Force in October 1943 and set up its HQ in the first week of November. Assigned to it were four medium Bombardment Groups previously controlled by the 3rd Bombardment Wing of the 8th Air Force, the 322nd BG at Andrews Field, the 323rd BG at Earls Colne, the 386th BG at Great Dunmow and the 387th BG at Chipping Ongar. During November two new Wings were formed: the 98th Bombardment Wing to control the 323rd and 387th BGs and the 99th BW to look after the 322nd and 386th Groups. Each Wing then absorbed two more Groups as they arrived in this country from training in the USA, and early in 1944 a third Wing, the 97th BW, was activated to control three more Groups which were then arriving. In addition, from February 1944, a Pathfinder Squadron (Provisional) and a Weather Reconnaissance Squadron were available, controlled directly by IX Bomber Command HQ, although as no provision had been made for these units in long-term plans personnel had to be drawn from other units in the Command.

For some time after the activation of IX Bomber Command, 8th Air Force HQ exercised sanctions over IX BC operations, as clearly all USAAF offensive missions had to be coordinated. IX BC's efforts were, however, directed toward a very different end than those of VIII Bomber Command. Whereas the 8th Air Force 'heavies' were tasked with destroying strategic targets

vital to the enemy war effort located, often, deep into Germany, IX BC's job was to provide a tactical bombing function, initially as a softening-up process in advance of an invasion of Europe and subsequently in support of the ground forces.

The two B-26 Wings carried on with this work through the transition period and were joined early in 1944 by the three A-20-equipped Groups of the 97th Bombardment Wing, fresh from the USA. These Groups found themselves at three Essex airfields: the 409th BG at Little Walden; the 410th BG at Birch and the 416 BG at Wethersfield. At much the same time four more B-26 Groups arrived from training in the United States and joined the two existing Bombardment Wings. The 344th BG went to Stansted and the 391st BG to Matching, both under the 99th Wing, while the 98th Wing absorbed the 394th BG at Boreham and the 397th BG at Rivenhall. When all these movements had been completed over 700 B-26s were located on Essex airfields, and IX Bomber Command controlled its full complement of eleven Groups. These Groups were fully in action during one week in May 1944, IX BC aircraft dropped more 2000lb bombs than during the six preceding months, an intense strain on the resources of IX AFSC, which had to provide the hardware.

Late in July 1944, the 98th CBW Groups began to move to airfields on or close to the south coast of England, the better to hit targets in Normandy, but the other CBWs stayed put until

Brig. Gen. Samuel E. Anderson visited Matching on 27 July 1944 to present awards to men of the 391st BG

[via R. Mynn]

moving direct to bases in France in August and September 1944. The 98th then rejoined the other two Wings, and all three, now retitled 9th Bombardment Division, played a vital part in the Allied advance across France and the Low Countries and into Germany, keeping up the intense pressure on tactical targets all the way. The end of the war in Europe was now in sight, but in February the first all-A-26 mission was flown. Scheduled to replace the B-26 and A-20, the A-26 had 75 miles greater range than the B-26 and 100 miles more than the A-20. The new aircraft was also highly adaptable to low-level bombing and strafing. The conversion of the 386th BG to the A-26 enabled a shortage of B-26s within the 98th BW to be overcome, and the 410th BG converted in May, but after a short active service period the A-26s were quickly redeployed to the Pacific area. The War over, 9th BD was, in May 1945, again retitled, becoming 9th Air Division. As such, its task long completed, it was inactivated on 20 November 1945.

'Bank Nite Betty' of the 397th BG   [B. Stait]

Components:	97th Bomb Wing		
	98th Bomb Wing		
	99th Bomb Wing		
Bases:	Marks Hall	6.11.43	
	Chartres (F)	18.9.44	
	Reims (F)	10.44	
	Namur (B)	4.45	— 20.11.45
Commanding Officers:	Maj. Gen. Samuel E. Anderson		
	Brig. Gen. Richard C. Sanders	24.5.45	
	Col. Reginald F. Vance	12.8.45	— 20.11.45

Cynical nose-art wording 'Sure Go For No Dough' on a 585th BS (394th BG) B-26   [via Bryan Jones]

Dual names 'Bootsie' and 'Paula E' were carried by this 416th BG A-20
[Merle Olmsted]

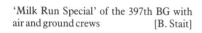

'Milk Run Special' of the 397th BG with air and ground crews   [B. Stait]

B-26B 131912 [FW:Q] 'Damd Fino' with crew chief and corporal, 387th BG   [G. Vasampaur via D. W. Crouchman]

IX FIGHTER COMMAND

Re-activated in England on 16 October 1943, IX Fighter Command's task was to inaugurate, equip and train tactical air commands, originally known as Air Support Commands, until they were ready to operate with the ground forces in the front line. IX Fighter Command thus had a finite life, and was planned to dissolve when its job was complete. At least six weeks training was to be provided to all combat units in lX FC to fit them for the enormous task ahead.

With the build-up well under way, IX ASC was activated in December 1943 and XIX ASC in January 1944, IX ASC taking most of the early-trained Groups, although the two ASCs were intended to be equal in strength eventually. By the end of January 1944 the ASCs had virtually taken over the function of

1X FC, which then became a crew-supply organisation, existing on paper rather than in fact.

However, late in February 1944 IX FC was brought back to life temporarily to operate in conjunction with the HQ of 11 Group, RAF, at Uxbridge. Administrative functions were carried out for IX FC by IX TAC, which was redesignated from IX ASC in April 1944.

During the period of movement of Fighter Groups from England to the Continent following the invasion of Europe, all Fighter Groups remaining in England were controlled through IX FC, but once the last Group had left, IX FC became inactive, remaining so for the remainder of the War.

Components:	70th Fighter Wing (1943/44)	
	71st Fighter Wing (1943/44)	
	84th Fighter Wing (1944)	
	l00th Fighter Wing (1943/44)	
	303rd Fighter Wing (1944)	
Bases:	Middle Wallop	30.11.43
Commanding Officers:	Maj. Gen. Elwood R. Quesada	18.10.43 — N/K

IX TACTICAL AIR COMMAND

Activated as IX Air Support Command on 4 December 1943, soon after the formation of the 9th Air Force, this Command was the first of the organisations parented and brought to strength by IX Fighter Command, which was responsible for initial training and supply functions. IX ASC became operational in its own right in February 1944 with four Fighter Wings, and carried on with IX FC's intensive campaign of attacks on tactical targets in northern France which was to lead up to the invasion in June. The command assumed its revised title of IX Tactical Air Command in April 1944 and shortly afterwards IX TAC personnel joined their RAF counterparts at a number of fighter control centres and DF Stations in southern England. As the date planned for the invasion neared, IX TAC's twelve Groups, including a Tactical Reconnaissance Group, were taking part in the systematic destruction of roads and bridges to thwart the enemy's re-supply efforts.

By D-Day, 6 June 1944, IX TAC's groups were poised to take part in the largest invasion ever mounted. The four Groups of the 70th Fighter Wing were based on coastal airfields in southern England, while 71st Fighter Wing's three Groups were located further inland on 'permanent' airfields; the 84th Fighter Wing's four Groups were also near the coast, two of them on Advanced Landing Grounds constructed for this operation. From these bases, aircraft of all the Command's Fighter Groups were able to protect effectively the huge cross-channel movement of shipping, wipe out coastal defences, cover troop landings on the beaches and prevent enemy reinforcements reaching the battle area. The IX TAC's 67th TRG, meanwhile, was kept at full pressure reporting on enemy movements and assessing battle damage.

As soon as airstrips built in Normandy by IX Engineer Command were ready, IX TAC Groups began to move to them. The first Group to leave England was the 371st FG, which arrived at

Beuzeville on 17 June and the 366th FG, which took up position at St. Pierre du Mont the same day. By the end of June another five FGs of the IX TAC, and a first Squadron of the 67th TRG had arrived, and the last of the other four Fighter Groups came in on 6 August.

Control of IX TAC and XIX TAC aircraft during Operation Overlord was initially carried out by controllers of the lst Air Combat Control Squadron on board ships, using radar and VHF radio, but once footholds on land had been established, IX TAC's 70th FW set up control facilities on the beach, and continued to operate from there until early August.

For the first seven weeks after D-Day, IX TAC maintained its intensive campaign against the enemy, in co-operation with ground forces. During that period, all available aircraft were sent on 22 June to take part in the massive attacks on Cherbourg, but it was found that the lack of mobile ground-to-air communication and of detailed knowledge of the area, coupled with very short notice of the operation, created one of the few errors of judgement in the application of tactical fighter-bombers in the whole campaign.

Said at the time to have been the most effective sustained close-support operation yet mounted, Operation Cobra, the attack on the St. Lo area on 25 July 1944 was a major task in which aircraft of IX TAC took part. The combined IX TAC/First Army operations centre co-ordinated the attack very successfully, and over the following two days the aircraft flew hundreds of sorties, claims of destruction or damage to enemy vehicles averaging 1000 per day. As no night-fighters were yet available, delayed-action bombs were dropped during daylight, causing 24-hour havoc at important road junctions and concentration points. Night bombing by radar-vectored P-38s was tried, but with limited success. It was quickly realised that the effectiveness of IX TAC, and the other TACs, was directly

Capt. Don M. Beerbower, a recipient of the Silver Star for gallantry in action in the cockpit of P-51B 312375, displaying 17 Swastikas and one locomotive, signifying the success of past missions

[via H. Holmes]

related to the efficiency of the communications system and of the available electronic aids, so considerable efforts were made to improve the procedures and equipment.

Determined to split the US First and Third Armies, the enemy attempted to counter-attack from Mortain, but IX TAC demonstrated that control of the airspace, providing reliable cover over army formations and the chance of attacking targets of opportunity, was effective both defensively and offensively. Fighter Groups of IX TAC, with XIX TAC and RAF participation, were able to strike against every target referred to them by the armies on the ground, repeatedly dispersing enemy troop concentrations preparing to counter-attack. The situation was highly volatile at the time, and some IX TAC Groups were put under the control of XIX TAC for a period. Both TACs, and the RAF, struck hard at enemy troop formations retreating from Falaise in mid-August, destroying huge numbers of German vehicles and turning the retreat into chaos.

Late in the summer of 1944, when the US Ninth Army moved into position, IX TAC provided some elements for the formation of XXIX TAC, whose task it would be to support Ninth Army forces. Then, in October, one of the two P-61-equipped night-fighter squadrons which had been assigned to IX ADC was transferred to IX TAC to enable it to switch to night intruder, rather than defence, operations. Excellent results were achieved, and it was felt that this tiny night-fighter

force should be expanded, but this plan never came to fruition.

So the relentless Allied advance over Europe continued, until on 16 December 1944 the German army launched a counter-offensive, in bad weather conditions, in the Ardennes forest of Belgium, with the object of isolating Allied forces pressurising the Siegfried Line. Communications became a problem, and to alleviate this IX TAC was transferred temporarily to British 2nd TAF control. Eventually the threat was dealt with and IX TAC continued to operate with the US First Army in the advance to the river Roer. First Army reached the Rhine on 2 March 1945 and crossed it over the Remagen bridge. On the other side, a determined counter-attack by enemy aircraft, including jetpropelled Me.262s, was repulsed by IX TAC Groups, which also once again took the offensive by attacking Luftwaffe airfields such as Lippe.

By now the end was in sight, and few important operations were carried out by IX TAC during the last couple of weeks of hostilities, apart from attacks on shipping off Flensburg in north Germany, from where it was rumoured that Nazi leaders might try to escape. By the first week of May 1945 nothing was left to attack, and offensive operations came to a halt.

After VE-Day, routine flying by IX TAC took place until September, and in October 1945 the Command left Europe to return to the United States.

Components:	70th Fighter Wing (1944/45)		
	71st Fighter Wing (1944)		
	84th Fighter Wing (1944)		
	100th Fighter Wing (1944)		
Bases:	Aldermaston Court	4.12.43	
	Middle Wallop	1.2.44	
	Uxbridge 15.2.44		
	Au Gay (F)	10.6.44	
	Les Obeaux (F)	2.7.44	
	Canisy (F)	2.8.44	
	Coulouvray (F)	12.8.44	
	Haleine (F)	22.8.44	
	Versailles (F)	2.9.44	
	Janoulx (B)	11.9.44	
	Verviers (B)	2.10.44	
	Bruhl (G)	26.3.45	
	Marburg (G)	8.4.45	
	Weimar (G)	26.4.45	
	Fritzlar (G)	26.6.45	— 9.45

Commanding Officers:	Col. Clarence E. Crumrine	4.12.43	
	Maj. Gen. Elwood R. Quesada	1.2.44	
	Brig. Gen. Ralph F. Stearley	21.4.44	— 9.45

'Sheaf's Jug', a P-47 displaying bomber-style nose-art on the engine cowling
[H. Holmes]

XII TACTICAL AIR COMMAND

Only a component of the 9th Air Force while attached to it for about six weeks, XII TAC had previously been part of the US 12th Air Force. It had worked closely with the US Seventh Army in its advance northward from the south of France, and, late in September 1944 came under 9th Air Force administrative and operational control. On 25 October 1944, 1st Tactical Air Force (Provisional) was constituted, and 9th Air Force then transferred the 71st Fighter Wing of three Groups, with support units, to XII TAC. It was mid-November, however, before 1st TAF took over responsibility and XII TAC passed out of the 9th Air Force.

Components:	71st Fighter Wing		
Bases:	(France)	9.44	—N/K
Commanding Officers:	Brig. Gen. Gordon P. Saville		

Following constitution as XIX Air Support Command in England at the end of November 1943, this second ASC was activated on 4 January 1944 and redesignated XIX Tactical Air Command on 18 April. A move to France, with 100th and 303rd Fighter Wings under its control, came in July 1944, and the Command was pronounced operational on 1 August, its task being to co-operate with the US Third Army. The new combined force went straight into action in the massive operation at St. Lo, followed by the task of clearing Britanny of remaining enemy forces, and threw its weight into the Falaise Gap, after which the Command, with the Third Army, raced across France toward the Siegfried Line. All this frenetic activity caused XIX TAC's HQ to be moved five times during its first month in France in order to keep up with the ground forces.

XIX TAC's range of operations became extended to more than 300 miles (480 km) between Brest in Britanny and Paris. On one particular day, XIX TAC Groups' aircraft were taking part in the Siege of Brest, covering armoured columns advancing toward Paris and guarding the US Third Army's flank along the river Loire. This latter task was carried out so effectively that when the local German commander surrendered he asked for Brig. Gen. Weyland, XIX TAC Commander, to be present at the formal capitulation on 7 September. During this period of widely-spread activities, it became necessary for XIX TAC HQ to split into four components: one to administer Groups in the area of the beach-head; a rear element to administer there; an advanced element to control all other Groups; and a small echelon to stay with the highly mobile Third Army HQ to provide constant liaison.

After assisting IX TAC Groups during the German counter-attack at Mortain, XIX TAC, like IX TAC, provided a nucleus for newly-activated XXIX TAC. Also similarly to IX TAC, XIX TAC absorbed a P-61 night fighter squadron, the 425th NFS,

for night intruder operations, which were deemed very effective. Later in October 1944, XIX TAC took on the job of breaching the Dieuze dam east of Nancy, and this proved highly successful. Very accurate bombing was required, so instead of the A-20s or B-26s of IX Bomber Command, P-47s of XIX TAC were employed, the first time that USAAF fighter-bombers had been used in the ETO for such a task.

After the counter-attack in the Ardennes, in which XIX TAC took little part, had been overcome, the Allied advance toward the Rhine speeded up. XIX TAC Groups helped at this stage by containing enemy troop concentrations as the US Third Army crossed the Prum, Saar and Moselle rivers. An effective subsiduary operation was mounted on 19 March 1945, when XIX TAC P-47s attacked the HQ of the German Commander-in-Chief in an old castle at Ziegenburg during the lunch hour. High explosive and napalm bombs put the complex completely out of action, much to the disgust of General von Runstedt, expressed during his interrogation.

The second crossing of the river Rhine was made by the US Third Army during the night of 22 March 1945, and next day XIX TAC aircraft were airborne from dawn to dusk providing cover and attacking any targets requested by Third Army Headquarters.

Unlike the other two TACs, XIX TAC carried on its offensive, co-operating with the Third Army in its advance toward Bavaria. The XIX TAC fighter-bombers now concentrated on destroying columns of retreating Germans and leading the Third Army toward final victory. During this short period, Groups from IX and XXIX TACs were under XIX TAC control, but by the first week of May 1945 there was nothing more for the TACs to do, and they therefore ceased operation. XIX TAC stayed in Germany for a further three months before returning to the United States in August 1945.

Components:	100th Fighter Wing		
	303rd Fighter Wing		
Bases:	Middle Wallop	4.1.44	
	Aldermaston Court	1.2.44	
	(France)	7.44	
	(Luxemburg)	1.45	
	(Germany)	4.45	−8.45
Commanding Officers:	Maj. Gen. Elwood R. Quesada	4.1.44	
	Col. Clarence E. Crumrine	1.2.44	
	Maj. Gen. Otto P. Weyland	4.2.44	
	Brig. Gen. Homer Sanders	23.5.45	
	Col. Roger J. Browne	5.7.45	−8.45

354th FG's P-47D 420473 taxies in at Rosieres-en-Haye in December 1944. The engine cowling is yellow, skull-and-crossbones and bald eagle are black; note GI on wing

XXIX TACTICAL AIR COMMAND

The only major Command of the 9th Air Force to come into being after, D-Day, XXIX TAC (Prov.) was activated in September 1944 to co-operate with the newly-formed US Ninth Army. XXIX TAC became operational on 2 October 1944, its nucleus having been provided by IX and XIX TACs and IX FC, which by then had virtually been dissolved. Initially four P-47 Groups, a Tactical Reconnaissance Group and a Liaison Squadron were assigned to the new Command.

The first major campaign involving XXIX TAC was in the Ardennes at the end of 1944, when the Germans made a heavy counter-attack against Allied forces advancing toward the Siegfried Line. During this period, the Ninth Army, and with it XXIX TAC, were temporarily handed over to the control of the British 2nd Tactical Air Force. When, during this counter-offensive, XXIX TAC HQ was in danger of being captured, a rear HQ, complete with duplicate communications equipment, was set up to provide continuity. At all times, XXIX TAC HQ was located close to that of the Ninth Army in order to achieve complete liaison. The principle of movement of the HQ leap-frog fashion was in fact followed by XXIX TAC during its entire existence.

When the Ninth Army resumed its advance, XXIX TAC followed suit, and on 22 February 1945 took part in Operation Clarion, a concentrated effort to destroy the entire German railway system, or what remained of it. Next day, when ground troops were crossing the river Rhine, XXIX TAC Groups participated by attacking everything that moved on the enemy side with bombs, rockets and machine guns. At the end of April 1945, XXIX TAC ceased offensive operations, flying reconnaissance and defensive sorties only from this point.

Components:	84th Fighter Wing		
	303rd Fighter Wing		
Bases:	(France)	9.44	—N/K
Commanding Officers:	Brig. Gen. Richard E. Nugent		

IX TROOP CARRIER COMMAND

IX TCC, activated in England on 16 October 1943, initially comprised a cadre of just six officers who were still in the United States. Before long, however, a Troop Carrier Wing of three Groups was transferred to the Command from the 8th Air Force, and rapid expansion got under way. By the end of January 1944 over 8500 personnel were allocated to Troop Carrier Command, and two months later 65 of the 161 units which would comprise the Command (not all of them flying units) had been activated.

All but one Troop Carrier Group used C-47 and/or C-53 aircraft, 353 of which had been taken on charge by the end of February 1944 and 1226 by the end of May. Each TCG was allocated 64 operational aircraft plus sixteen in reserve, and two combat crews 'owned' each aircraft.

With the forthcoming invasion of Europe the sole reason for its existence, IX TCC organised a comprehensive series of exercises to ready the crews for their task. These comprised paratroop drops, glider tow-offs and landings using the Waco CG-4, the glider most widely used by IX TCC, air landing of supplies, and casualty evacuation, the three Command and thirty-eight Wing exercises carried out culminating in Operation Eagle, the full-scale invasion practice held on 12 May 1944.

To achieve absolute accuracy of navigation, a pathfinder school was organised by IX TCC headquarters on 1 March 1944, and intensive training was given to selected crews in all aspects of day and night navigation and the use of all the available electronic devices which would enable navigators to determine their position accurately.

These exercises proved to have been highly worthwhile when the day of the invasion at last arrived. Early on the morning of 6 June 1944, the aircraft of all fourteen TCGs, preceded by nineteen pathfinder C-47s, left their English bases to become part of an armada of USAAF and RAF aircraft carrying paratroops and equipment to Normandy. Many dropped their passengers in the St. Mere Eglise area and returned to base to pick up more troops. In addition, 104 C-47s of the 434th and 437th TCGs, all towing CG-4A gliders packed with troops of the 82nd and 101st

Enlisted men loading ammunition boxes onto a C-47 at Spanhoe
[R. Baker via D. Benfield]

Maj. David E. Daniel, CO of the 87th TCS, 438th TCG, seen with his aircraft, 2100738, which displayed some interesting nose-art

[Lt. Col. D. E. Daniel via D. Benfield]

Airborne Divisions, made their way across the English Channel successfully. By about 04.00 hours, when the last troops were dropped in the early phase of the operation, the TCGs had made 821 sorties, during which sixteen aircraft were lost to the enemy defences.

Late in the evening of the same day, 32 C-47s of the 434th TCG, towing Horsa gliders this time, delivered more men of the 101st Airborne Division, while C-47s from the 435th, 436th, 437th and 438th TCGs, 176 in total, towed a mixture of CG-4 and Horsa gliders carrying reinforcement troops of the 82nd Division. Early next morning, another 292 C-47s hauling CG-4s or Horsas made the crossing with men of the 82nd AD. This time the 434th, 435th, 437th, 439th and 441st TCGs were involved, but the 436th TCG was the Group which carried out twenty-four re-supply missions over the next six days.

The invasion and subsequent airborne supply roles successfully accomplished, it was possible to release some elements of the Command for other tasks. On 10 July 1944, 50th and 53rd Troop Carrier Wings were detached to Italy to participate in the invasion of southern France, and thus temporarily passed out of IX TCC control. Then, the 1st Allied Airborne Army was activated to control any further paradropping or glider-towing operations which might be required, and on 1 September 1944 IX Troop Carrier Command was re-assigned to United States Strategic Air Force for administration and to 1st AAA for operational control. For the sake of completing the picture, however, it is felt appropriate to continue the story of the erstwhile IX TCC in this Chapter and of its constituent Groups in Chapter 4.

Almost immediately after the transfer of control came the Arnhem operation in which between 17 and 23 September 1944 all fourteen TCGs played their part by dropping US and British paratroops and later by towing CG-4 gliders carrying troop reinforcements and supplies. Once again the 82nd and 101st Airborne Divisions were the troops carried, and all told 1899 glider/tug combinations were towed from thirteen English bases.

The final major operation for the TCGs was the crossing of the river Rhine, Operation Varsity, on 24 March 1945, and this time double-tows were employed, most tugs being C-47s, each hauling two CG-4s. Allied occupation of Continental airfields enabled this operation to be mounted from France. In all, 610 tugs towed 906 gliders to the Wesel area to enable the final push into Germany to proceed. This was the first operation in which the C-46 Commando aircraft carried paratroops into combat, but this aircraft was found to be much more likely to catch fire after being hit than the C-47, partly due to lack of self-sealing fuel tanks. The C-46 carried twice the number of troops than the C-47, thus reducing the potential casualty rate among crew members by half, but it was not able to carry full equipment for the troops it could contain. During this operation, a number of the larger CG-13A gliders were used for the first time, towed by C-46s.

After the end of hostilities, the TCGs carried out a general transport function, at the same time reducing in number by de-activation or return to the United States. By the end of 1945 only three Groups remained, and these ceased operation early in 1946.

Components:	50th Troop Carrier Wing		
	52nd Troop Carrier Wing		
	53rd Troop Carrier Wing		
Bases:	Cottesmore	16.10.43	
	Grantham (St. Vincents)	1.12.43	
	Ascot (Sunninghill Park)	20.9.44	—5.9.45
Commanding Officers:	Brig. Gen. Benjamin F. Giles	16.10.43	
	Maj. Gen. Paul L. Williams	25.2.44	—12.7.45

'Forty Niners' nose-art on an aircraft of the 49th TCS, 313th TCG
[Rose via D. Benfield]

Unloading some of the first wounded troops to be returned to the UK after D-Day by 9th Air Force C-47 [D. Benfield]

US military nurses assisting in the loading of casualties into a IX TCC C-47   [P. J. Johansen via D. Benfield]

C-47s in formation over Portland Bill before D-Day   [D. Benfield]

CG-4A gliders ready to be towed off a temporary airstrip near Eindhoven in Holland for possible further use

[D. Benfield]

A Waco CG-4A glider, by far the most numerous glider type used by United States airborne troops in the battle for Europe.　　　[via D. Benfield]

Troops of the 82nd Airborne Division about to board Horsa gliders at Upottery on 7 June 1944. Thirty Horsas and twenty CG-4As were towed to St. Mere Eglise that day   [Col. Young via D. Benfield]

The remains of a C-47 written off by an exploding grenade at Spanhoe were used later, in conjunction with a water tank, for survival training
[R. Baker via D. Benfield]

The remains of a Waco CG-4A glider after operational use. This shot illustrated the five sections in which the crated aircraft was delivered for assembly
[IWM neg. OWIL70849]

Although it provided an absolutely vital contribution to the 9th Air Force's campaign, little recognition has been given to the enormous efforts made by the IX AFSC. This chapter is an attempt to rectify that state of affairs, by means of a brief summary of the Command's activities.

Originally entitled IX Air Service Command, the Command had seen service with the 9th Air Force in Egypt, and was re-formed in England on the same day, 16 October 1943. The new Commanding Officer was Maj. Gen. Henry J. Miller and, apart from a few men who arrived from Egypt, personnel were drawn from VIII AFSC and VIII Tactical Air Service Area Command. On the day of formation the Command moved from Bushy Park to Sunninghill House at Ascot, which was destined to be its HQ for many months. As personnel and facilities built up, IX ASC was able to develop a structure to provide the planned comprehensive maintenance, assembly, modification and repair service needed by the 9th Air Force. During the first few weeks, for example, modification kits fitted included a water injection system for P-47s, alterations to P-47 canopies to assist jettisoning, P-51 gunsights and the adaption of B-26 aircraft as target tugs. At the same time, personnel were being instructed in the repair and maintenance of Horsa gliders. Initially, IX ASC administered several different types of unit, mostly down a chain of command. These units can be summarised thus:

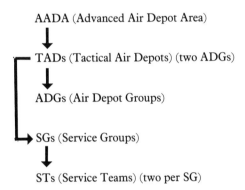

AADA (Advanced Air Depot Area)

TADs (Tactical Air Depots) (two ADGs)

ADGs (Air Depot Groups)

SGs (Service Groups)

STs (Service Teams) (two per SG)

Soon, however, TADs found it difficult to administer the SGs, so AADA began to control SGs direct, although nominal control remained with the TADs. AADA was, in December 1943, split into 1st AADA, with HQ at Haseley Court, Oxfordshire, and 2nd AADA, HQd at Arborfield Cross in Berkshire. 1st AADA now controlled 1st, 2nd and 3rd TADs, while 2nd AADA was in charge of 4th, 5th and 6th TADs.

The six TADs were formed in November 1943, though the title TAD was nothing more than a means of defining a grouping of two ADGs. A TAD did not have a CO or adjutant, and each ADG ran independently, although in times of need equipment and manpower might be pooled. Bases and tasks for the TADs can be summarised as follows, details shown being the situation in August 1944.

1st TAD, North Witham
   29th and 33rd ADGs
   10th, 49th, 78th, 82nd, 100th, 317th and 318th SGs
     Maintained C-47s, C-53s, CG-4As and Horsas of IX TCC
2nd TAD, Stansted
   30th and 91st ADGs
   42nd, 53rd, 70th and 304th SGs
     Maintained B-26s of IX BC
3rd TAD, Grove
   43rd and 45th ADGs
   4th, 30th and another SGs
     Maintained Spitfires, A-20s, F-6s, L-4s, L-5s, P-51As, P-61s and any other types not specifically assigned

4th TAD, Kingston Bagpuize
   2nd and 42nd ADGs
   9th, 309th and 312th SGs
     Maintained F-5s, P-38s and P-51B/Cs
5th TAD, Chilbolton
   10th and 86th ADGs
   83rd, 84th and 327th SGs
     Maintained P-47s
6th TAD, Membury
   7th and 16th ADGs
   26th, 32nd, 74th and 326th SGs
     Maintained P-47s

A typical TAD of two ADGs comprised the following units:
   2 HQs and HQ Squadrons
   2 Repair Squadrons
   2 Supply Squadrons
   2 QM Truck Companies
   2 QM Platoons
   2 Ordnance Medium Maintenance Companies
   2 Mobile Repair & Reclamation Squadrons (on attachment)
   1 Medical Supply Platoon
   1 Signal Company (Aviation)
   1 Ordnance Depot Company
   1 MP Company
   1 Station Complement Squadron

In practice, if required, an Ordnance Ammunition Company and/or a Chemical Depot Company would be added. The Station Complement Squadron's function was that of housekeeping, air traffic control, etc. The Service Groups, while assigned to ADGs, were generally attached to combat units. They were the basic unit for supply, maintenance and repair of aircraft on established airfields, and each was divided into two Service Teams, one per combat Group. Each SG comprised:
   2 Service Squadrons for aircraft maintenance
   1 QM Truck Company
   2 Ordnance Supply & Maintenance Companies
   1 Signal Company (for maintenance of airborne radio etc.)
   1 Chemical Company
   1 QM Company.(for general supply and salvage work)

Another major component of IX ASC was BADA (Base Air Depot Area), which was formed late in October 1943. A site at Baverstock, near Dinton in Wiltshire, was selected in December to be the location for BADA, which would be the receiving point for all 9th Air Force supplies as well as the command HQ for intransit depots, BADs, aircraft assembly depots and the ammunition depot at Groveley Wood. Storage space was to become a formidable problem at Baverstock, where 470050 sq. ft. of closed and 311200 sq.ft. of open storage was eventually provided.

Vitally important to the success of IX AFSC's activities were the Mobile Repair & Reclamation Squadrons (MR&RS), which were formed in November 1943 to carry out off-airfield work and to assist in any maintenance or assembly tasks as directed. Each Squadron comprised nine self-supporting Teams, and for administration the MR&RS were attached to Service Groups. Equipment issued to each MR&RS usually consisted of a 6x6 truck, often with a crane attachment for dealing with engine changes or salvage work in the field, one or two jeeps, a field cooking range, tents and a variety of tools. Thus provided, the twenty or so men in each Team were ready to tackle any job which might come their way. Some MR&RS found themselves devoted to dealing with one type of aircraft for a period of time or assisting with the servicing of aircraft of one particular Group.

Several of the MR&RS, which were usually under the overall control of an ADG, moved to Normandy very soon after D-Day, and lived and worked in the same field conditions as the ground troops. As the 9th Air Force advanced over France and beyond, so did the MR&RS, sometimes with a change of function on the way as the campaign developed. Finally, after a period of work on salvage and storage, the MR&RS, now depleted in personnel, were inactivated at about the same time as the 9th Air Force itself.

It will be seen that many of the MR&RS were formed at Matching before quickly moving elsewhere. Matching housed, in the autumn of 1943, the 13th Replacement Control Depot (RCD), a pool of men from which the nucleus of an MR&RS was created. Unfortunately, the historical records of some of the Squadrons are lacking in quality and/or quantity, which explains the gaps in the brief histories given in Appendix E.

For assembly of aircraft for the 9th Air Force arriving at the main entry point, Avonmouth docks, near Bristol, a site at Filton airfield was chosen in December 1943. It was operational in eight weeks, and three MR&RS were drafted in to carry out the assembly work, under very difficult conditions. Similar circumstances could be found at Crookham Common, adjacent to Greenham Common airfield, where the huge Glider Assembly Depot was set up.

The first gliders for IX TCC had been assembled at Aldermaston by British civilian workers, but they were completely untrained and only succeeded in ruining 72 gliders. The decision was therefore taken to set up the Assembly Depot, and by December 1943 200 gliders had been completed there, although IX TCC would not at first accept them, as they did not know which operations they were for or how many would be needed. That month, 600 gliders were ordered for completion by 1 January 1944, but only 180 were finished by that date due to severe under-planning of the labour involved.

By mid-January 1944 good progress had been made in assigning and training IX ASC personnel, although there were some shortages of skilled men. Some of the shortfalls were made up by transfers from the 8th Air Force. Work on facilities which would be needed in future included the modification of 250 trailers for use as field offices, the construction of 21 airfield control vehicles and 10 glider-borne workshops. There were the inevitable shortages of equipment, particularly of fork-lift trucks and 2½-ton trucks. On the engineering side, those men attempting to build the many depots which would soon be required found a severe shortage of building materials and of local labour, so US troops were drafted in to help. Delays in procuring land added to the problem, as did the overloaded railway system. Water supply and sewage disposal problems also had their effect.

IX ASC was retitled IX AFSC on 29 January 1944, and VIII Air Force Intransit Depot Group (IDG), based at Wapley Common, became part of BADA, less personnel and equipment. This Group was divided into three Beach Squadrons, two Port Squadrons, two Air Transit Squadrons and a HQ unit. The Beach Squadrons were trained to operate just behind the beaches which would eventually be used for the forthcoming invasion of France, while the other squadrons handled material arriving from the USA at ports and airfields. Detachments were located at Southampton, Bristol, London and St. Mellons in South Wales.

At the end of January 1944 the personnel strength of IX AFSC was 2964 officers and 41880 enlisted men. Shortage of space, particularly at the Glider Assembly Depot, was still proving a problem, and IX TCC was asked to expedite the removal of completed gliders. Experiments made by IX AFSC personnel at this time included the evaluation of war-weary B-17s and B-24s to determine their cargo, fuel and passenger-carrying potential. Other work included the fitting of prototype installations of OBOE in B-26 aircraft and GEE in C-47s.

So the build-up of IX AFSC continued. The Command was likened at the time to a collosal business empire comprising a mail-order house, a commercial airline, an arsenal, a garage, a drug factory, a road transport system and a personnel centre all rolled into one. More units added in March 1944 included an

Aircraft Replacement Centre at Mullaghmore in Northern Ireland, which very soon moved to nearby Greencastle. There, at least ten aircraft stood ready for collection at all times. In May, another ARC opened at Snailwell in Cambridgeshire, specialising in A-20 aircraft. During July, however, the ARC at Greencastle was passed to another Command.

Brig. Gen. Myron R. Wood took over as CO of IX AFSC from Maj. Gen. Miller on 6 May 1944, and further alterations to the Command followed. On 17 May BADA was dissolved, and its constituent parts taken over by other agencies; the Aircraft Assembly Depot at Filton and BAD were absorbed by USSTAF; the Glider Assembly Depot at Crookham Common, still working hard, became part of 1st AADA; 2nd AADA took over the Ammunition Supply Depot; and IX AFSC HQ took the Intransit Depot Group.

As an indication of the rapidly-increasing size and effectiveness of IX AFSC, the following figures can be quoted:

	Nov. 1943	March 1944
Aircraft serviced	730	3631
Aircraft modified	97	527
Aircraft assembled	nil	173
Aircraft repaired	84	565
Gliders assembled	60	110
Truck ton-miles covered		663000
Cargo air-freighted (lbs)	12000	842000
Air ton-miles	748	72763
Aircraft ferried	3	678
Number of IX AFSC installations	22	67
Total IX AFSC personnel	20424	58503

Before long, aircraft and gliders assembled greatly exceeded these figures.

By now, plans for the invasion of Europe were well advanced and the part to be played by IX AFSC was well-defined. The first AFSC personnel to reach the beach-head would be men of the IDG Beach Squadrons, attached to Army Engineer Special Brigades to identify and segregate the supplies, ammunition and fuel. Next, QM Truck Companies would be landed to carry the material to the landing strips which the IX EC had created to be used for refuelling and rearming tactical aircraft. Airdrome Squadrons would man the airstrips, holding a few basic spares pending the arrival of well-equipped Service Squadron teams.

Detachment 'B' of IDG duly landed on D+1 under fire, and much of the successful organisation of 9th Air Force supply dumps in the early days was due to them. Work started as soon as possible on the salvage of re-useable glider parts and the remainder was burnt. IX AFSC HQ Detachment 'A' began to leave Ascot for France on D-Day, Detachment 'B' following ten days later, Detachment 'C' on 22 June and, finally, Detachment 'D' on 10 July. 2nd AADA was now combined with IX AFSC HQ to form IX AFSC Advanced HQ, which was set up in tents on D+3 near Cricqueville. On 14 July, however, Advanced HQ moved to a new site near Le Cambe, where the officers were billeted in a chateau at Jucoville which had until recently been the local Gestapo HQ. By the end of July, seven Service Groups and three Air Depot Groups, all of which had been administered by 2nd AADA, had arrived in France.

During July 1944, 302nd Air Transport Wing HQ was formed to control the 31st ATG, IX AFSC's vital passenger and cargo 'airline', and to be responsible for all air transport for the Command. Three airstrips in France were put under the jurisdiction of the 302nd ATW: A-21C at St Laurent-sur-Mer, A-22C at Coleville and A-24 at Biniville, all of which could accommodate C-47s. Colleville became more active than New York's La Guardia airport, handling a landing every three minutes on average. All passenger traffic was handled there, plus a great deal of cargo, while Biniville was used purely for casualty evacuation. To enlarge the 302nd ATW at this time, USSTAF made two squadrons of the 8th Air Force's 27th ATG available to it as required. The system of handling transport aircraft having been settled, it was found that many flights were not being cleared through 302nd ATW and some pilots were not filing flight plans, so that the situation became hazardous. This state of affairs was not allowed to continue.

In July 1944 it was agreed that USSTAF would make any necessary modifications to aircraft for the 9th Air Force except those already in TADs, and would store and allocate all aircraft except the 21 A-20s at 3rd TAD and 56 B-26s at 2nd TAD. USSTAF would also assemble all aircraft for 9th Air Force except L-4s and L-5s and store and allocate all non-operational aircraft. IX AFSC HQ moved to the chateau at Fengeres, near Periers on the Cherbourg peninsula, on 10 August 1944 but did not stay long, moving on again on 28 August. This time the staff found themselves in houses built before the war for workers at the Gnome-Rhone factory at Le Mans.

A further step forward came in August with the formation of Air Terminal Area teams to operate the large terminals in France. Maintenance of these airstrips was becoming a problem, so platoons of IX EC were brought in to carry out remedial work. 302nd ATW was still expanding rapidly; during the first ten days of August it flew 604 aircraft from England to France, although 40 of the Wing's assigned 65 crews were on loan to IX TCC. A typical day in the Wing's life was 29 August, when 84 tons of supplies and 92 passengers were flown from Grove to France and 73 wounded troops were brought back. Within France that day, 22 courier trips were flown carrying 29 passengers and 39 tons of freight.

During the same month, the VIII IDG was disbanded and 1st IDG formed in its place. The new IDG comprised a HQ, the 1st Air Intransit Depot Squadron and the 1st, 2nd, 3rd and 4th Port IDSs. Glider assembly recommenced at the huge Depot at Crookham Common, which was now staffed by 26 officers and 900 enlisted men. The new target was 700 gliders in 20 days, as IX TCC had asked for these before 1 September plus 1000 more during September. About 1300 gliders were already in completed state at Crookham Common, leaving 400 to be built. Empty crates in which the gliders sections had been sent from the USA were a huge problem which was solved by sending them to BADA at Baverstock for despatch to France, where timber and plywood were urgently needed. To accommodate the enormous number of gliders awaiting despatch, Greenham Common airfield was now put into use as an extra storage area.

The 302nd ATW was transferred to USSTAF control on 1 September 1944, with the exception of a cargo and mail-carrying squadron which now came under the control of a new 1st ATG (Prov.). On 5 September, with the transfer of IX TCC from 9th Air Force to 1st Allied Airborne Army jurisdiction, one TAD and seven SGs formerly controlled by 1st AADA left IX AFSC. At the same time, five MR&RSs were attached to Field Artillery units of the US Army to deal with their L-4 and L-5 aircraft. Later in the month, on 20 September, IX AFSC moved again, this time to Creil, near Paris, where the last few members from Ascot arrived at the same time.

Yet more changes of Station took place in October 1944, when those units of IX AFSC which had for six weeks or so been servicing the aircraft of XII TAC were transferred with that Command to USSTAF. Winterization of 9th Air Force aircraft and airstrips now became a vital task, involving the provision of cockpit covers, the use of alcohol in water-injection systems, and the ordering of large quantities of British snow-clearing machines. For the liaison aircraft of 9th Air Force and the FA, skis had to be ordered.

By the end of October 1944, 92% of IX AFSC personnel had left England for the Continent, including a few stragglers from Ascot who arrived on 10 November. As early as this, and ignorant of several major problems to come, IX AFSC had been detailed to prepare plans for the disarmament of Germany, pending the setting-up of a Disarmament Command in January 1945. In the event, Disarmament Command was set up in England, but immediately scrapped, and a Disarmament Division was set up within IX AFSC instead.

In December 1944 Continental Air Depot Area (CADA) was established in France on the pattern of the erstwhile BADA in England. That month, an extra task undertaken by IX AFSC units was the inspection of the 9th Air Force's 94 UC-78 aircraft. One of these useful machines, variously known as 'Bamboo Bomber' or 'Rhapsody in Glue', had crashed at Beauvais when wing fabric had peeled off. Many had in fact been modified on the production line, but several which had not were judged not worth repairing.

The heavy workload on IX AFSC continued, and in February 1945 included a request from 9th Bombardment Division that fifteen A-20Js or Ks be provided for a night bombing project entitled 'Firefly Little'. This project was, however, cancelled in April. By March the intense activity towards the final conquest of Germany created shortages of many materials and items of equipment but issues to the IX AFSC units was the highest ever.

By April 1945, the last full month of the war in Europe, disarmament teams for IX AFSC were taking over former Luftwaffe airfields and other bases at a rapidly-increasing rate. The programme was one of primary evaluation, followed by disposition of facilities, records, weapons, equipment, supplies and personnel who might not have fled. During the month the 1st ATG at Creil was designated as the point of entry for all 9th Air Force replacement aircraft, but it was not to be long before the demand was greatly reduced. All service units assigned to 1st TAF were re-assigned to IX AFSC in May, control to be exercised by 1st TAF SC(Prov.).

Then came the beginning of the great reduction in manpower and units following the successful end of hostilities. Unlike most combat units, IX AFSC could not just pack up and go home — there was still a huge task to carry out. Organised very quickly was a Personnel Control Depot, formed to process 300 men per day from disbanded units and to re-assign them or send them onward for demobilisation. Movement of aircraft, mainly A-26s, to the Pacific area via the USA began soon after VE-Day at the rate of 15 per day. All P-47s and P-51s with less than 200 airframe hours were moved to Creil for storage, while F-5s and F-6s with few hours began to leave for the Pacific. For the time being, all B-26s were retained in Europe, as were 500 C-47s, the remainder leaving for the Pacific area. Also destined to stay in Europe for a time were 960 B-17s of the 8th Air Force, some of which were used for a European mapping project, and 600 gliders, of which 200 were sold to the RAF, although why the RAF would want them is anybody's guess. By the end of June plans had been made for the storage of 400 B-17s, 600 B-26s and 1000 fighters on four airfields, which were manned by two Service Groups.

Disarmament reached its most active period in June 1945 and then declined. The 302nd ATW returned to IX AFSC control that month, as did many other units which then came together as 9th BADA at Erding in Germany. This organisation then began to carry out, on a vastly reduced scale, supply and maintenance functions up to and beyond the inactivation of the 9th Air Force in December 1945.

Truly amazing feats of organisation and action were carried out by IX AFSC in its two years or so of activity, without which the 9th Air Force could not have functioned.

Bases:	Sunninghill Hose, Ascot	16.11.43	
	Cricqueville (F)	9.6.44	
	Le Cambe (F)	14.7.44	
	Fengeres (F)	10.8.44	
	Le Mans (F)	28.8.44	
	Creil (F)	20.9.44	
	Luxemburg	1.5.45	— N/K
Commanding Officers:	Maj. Gen. Henry J. Miller	16.11.43	
	Brig. Gen. Myron R. Wood	6.5.44	— N/K

IX ENGINEER COMMAND

Well before the re-formation of the 9th Air Force, plans had been made to form an engineer division within VIII Air Support Command, but when it became clear that at least twenty thousand aviation engineer troops would be required for operation in the ETO, it was decided that an independent Engineer Command would be appropriate. For such a Command there was no precedent, and there was a certain amount of opposition to it. However, a headquarters was set up at the end of 1943, with sanction to proceed with the initial training of personnel and with planning for participation in Operation Overlord, the invasion of Europe.

During February 1944, the HQ, still not a fully-fledged Command, completed training of its first four battalions and received another four. Materials and equipment arrived, at a rather slower pace than desirable, but a major benefit soon accrued from the use of signals equipment sanctioned by HQ 9th Air Force, thus avoiding many communications problems. A number of light transport aircraft were also allocated, providing rapid movement of key personnel and enabling prospective airstrip sites to be surveyed from the air.

It was not until 30 March 1944 that IX EC was formally activated, and then only provisionally. By D-Day, IX EC comprised a Headquarters with its HQ Squadron, one camouflage battalion, three airborne engineer aviation battalions, four aviation regiment HQs, sixteen engineer aviation battalions and four

combat communications teams, plus all the usual support units, altogether represented by 17000 officers and enlisted men. The Command's task was a simple but vital and arduous one: to build and maintain airfields and airstrips in France from D-Day for the use of 9th Air Force Groups and then to follow very closely behind the advancing Armies, building more airfields as required. As the advance continued, an additional commitment was to be the refurbishment of captured enemy airfields. The plans involved the construction of two ELSs on D-Day itself; two R&R airstrips to be operational by midday on D+3; five ALGs to be ready for use at 06.00 on D+8, including the two erstwhile R&R strips; and three more ALGs to be in use on D+14.

IX EC moved to France in five stages, the first on D-Day, the second on D+5, and the last, which stayed in the UK to operate that end of the supply line, early in September 1944. Construction of airstrips just behind the Normandy beach-heads proceeded apace, the first one being operational at 21.15 on D-Day. Water supply lines and road repair were other vital tasks which fell to IX EC personnel at this time. During the first three months in France, IX EC engineers used 62034 rolls of steel mesh track, 723510 PSPs (pierced steel planks) and 42561 rolls of hessian matting, almost all of which was shipped from the UK, in all about 700 tons per day.

As Allied troops advanced over France toward Paris and the

Heavy plant in use by Engineer Aviation
Battalions in England   [D. Benfield]

Heavy plant in use by Engineer Aviation
Battalions in England   [D. Benfield]

east, IX EC became more and more extended, creating a number of communication problems. These were partly remedied by the activation of two Engineer Aviation Brigades on 1 August 1944 in an effort to decentralise control. The Brigades were then located close to the TACs and Armies they supported. To add to these difficulties, the coming of extremely wet-weather in September greatly restricted the Command's efforts to provide bases for the TAC Groups close to the front line. Sites being converted into airstrips became so muddy that instead of the normal hessian mat runway surface much heavier forms of construction had to be used. Sometimes this took the form of a hardcore foundation, but in less crucial cases perforated steel planking was found to be adequate. By mid-September, fifty airfields had been finished, with another eighteen under construction, ten of which were already being used.

A third Engineer Aviation Brigade was formed in September 1944, partly from the 1st and 2nd EABs and partly from units in the UK, to carry out work at the rear of the advancing forces, and this Brigade employed a large number of civilians. Later, the 3rd EAB was tasked with maintenance of airfields in the area west of the river Rhine.

As IX EC Headquarters near Paris found itself losing touch with Advanced HQ 9th Air Force, and with its Brigades in the field, an advanced and a rear HQ were set up in October 1944. This arrangement had the effect of putting intense pressure on IX EC's resources. Further alterations to the Command structure were then made. Following the formation of engineer commands within USSTAF and First TAF, IX EC provided assistance in setting up operating procedures and construction guidelines, but in November all the units of the two new Commands were placed under IX EC for supply and administration functions. Furthermore, IX EC provided a Brigade to First TAF EC for the construction of airfields in the Nancy area.

More confusion was to come. In February 1945 USSTAF assumed control of all aviation engineer troops in Europe, and IX EC's rear HQ became the HQ of the new organisation. The advanced HQ of IX EC then became its main HQ and began to be responsible for construction and repair of airfields for all three 9th Air Force TACs and for those of First TAF. Administration was now carried out by USSTAF EC but operational decisions were still firmly under the control of IX EC's own Headquarters.

This was the organisational system which saw the end of the war in Europe, but at that point IX EC became completely detached from USSTAF and was now once more totally under 9th Air Force control. From a peak personnel strength of 23000 during the rapid advance across France and into Germany the Command was now begining to shrink. Over the next few months vital repairs and alterations were made by IX EC on captured German airfields to ready them for use by the American forces of occupation, after which the multiplicity of units making up IX EC either disbanded or were absorbed into the peacetime structure of the occupation force. Without the incredible versatility of the men in the field and the efficiency of the supply organisation, the vital task carried out by IX EC units would have been impossible and the Second World War might well have been prolonged.

IX AIR DEFENCE COMMAND

Although planned from an early date, IX ADC, for which there was no precedent, was slow in being activated. The organisation of the new command was evolved by the then AA Officer of the 8th Air Force, Brig. Gen. W.L. Richardson, who spent several weeks with the fledgling IX ADC before returning on a more permanent basis at the end of 1944.

The development of IX ADC began when, in January 1944, one AAA Brigade and one AA Group were allocated to the 9th Air Force. These units were temporarily designated Air Defence HQ of the 9th Air Force, which then assumed control of all units employed in the defence of 9th AF airfields in the United Kingdom. IX ADC came into being at the end of March 1944 and was fully activated in May. Attached to it were up to eight AAA Brigades; the 71st Fighter Wing; the 422nd and 425th Night Fighter Squadrons; two signal air warning battalions; and two fighter control squadrons. As available US units were inadequate, two sectors of 85 Group, RAF, were attached for operations, and included fighter control and night fighter units.

To create a cohesive Command, a tactical training area was set up in England, where fighter, early warning and AAA units were given practice in the parts they would be called upon to play after the invasion of Europe. Training continued until 20 June 1944, when IX ADC's advanced HQ was set up in Normandy, and by 28 July the entire Command was in France, and the night fighter squadrons were under local control.

IX ADC units followed the Allied advance across France, but bureaucratic squabbles prompted the setting-up on 19 January 1945 of the Army Group Rear Air Boundary, the Army being responsible for the air defence of all installations forward of that line and IX ADC for installations to the rear.

When the end of the War arrived in May 1945, IX ADC was headquartered in Paris, but soon moved into Germany, where it remained on the de-activation of 9th Air Force in December 1945.

Components:	71st Fighter Wing (ex IX FC)		
Bases:	Hampstead	1.7.44	
	Ecrammeville (F)	7.44	
	Rennes (F)	25.8.44	
	Versailles (F)	8.9.44	
	Paris (F)	16.12.44	
	Neustadt (G)	25.5.45	
Commanding Officers:	Brig. Gen. William L. Richardson	1.7.44	
	Brig. Gen. Ned Schramm	28.7.44	
	Brig. Gen. William L. Richardson	27.10.44	—2.12.45

Another 404th FG P-47D was 227229 [7J:M]   [Merle Olmsted]

CHAPTER 3: THE WINGS

50th TROOP CARRIER WING

Constituted as 50th Transport Wing		8.1.41	
Activated		14.1.41	
Redesignated 50th Troop Carrier Wing as part of I TCC		7.42	
Moved to England to join IX TCC		9.43/10.43	
Returned to USA		9.45	
Components:	439th TCG		
	440th TCC		
	441st TCG		
	442nd TCG		
Bases:	Cottesmore	17.10.43	
	Bottesford	18.11.43	
	Exeter	26.4.44	
	Le Mans (F)	1.10.44	
	Chartres (F)	3.11.44	—29.9.45
Commanding Officers:	Brig. Gen. Julian M. Chappell		

52nd TROOP CARRIER WING

Constituted as 52nd Transport Wing		30.5.42	
Activated		15.6.42	
Redesignated 52nd Troop Carrier Wing		7.42	
Served with 12th Air Force in Mediterranean area			
Moved to England to join IX TCC		2.44/3.44	
Returned to USA		6.45/7.45	
Components:	313th TCG		
	314th TCG		
	315th TCG		
	316th TCG		
	61st TCG		
Bases:	Cottesmore	17.2.44	
	Amiens (F)	5.3.45	—20.6.45
Commanding Officers:	Brig. Gen. Harold L. Clark		

53rd TROOP CARRIER WING

Constituted		27.7.42	
Activated		1.8.42	
Moved to England to join IX TCC		1.44/3.44	
Returned to USA		10.45	
Components:	434th TCG		
	435th TCG		
	436th TCG		
	437th TCG		
	438th TCG		
Bases:	Greenham Common	11.3.44	
	Voisenon (F)	20.2.45	—10.45
Commanding Officers:	Brig. Gen. Maurice M. Beach		

70th FIGHTER WING

Constituted		11.8.43	
Activated		15.8.43	
Moved to England to join IX FC		11.43	
Remained in Europe after de-activation of 9th Air Force			
Components:	48th FG		
	67th TRG		
	354th FG		
	357th FG		
	358th FG		
	362nd FG		
	363rd FG		
	365th FG		
	366th FG		
	367th FG		
	368th FG		
	370th FG		
	371st FG		
	474th FG		
Bases:	Greenham Common	29.11.43	
	Boxted	6.12.43	
	Ibsley	17.4.44	
	Criqueville (F)	9.6.44	
	Villedieu-les-Poeles (F)	4.8.44	
	Le Teilleul (F)	16.8.44	
	Aillieres (F)	22.8.44	
	Versailles (F)	31.8.44	
	Marchais (F)	10.9.44	
	Liege (B)	3.10.44	
	Verviers (B)	22.1.45	
	Bruhl (G)	18.3.45	
	Bad Wildungen (G)	30.5.45	
	Furstenfeldbruck (G)	28.7.45	
	Neubiberg (G)	10.11.45	
Commanding Officers:	Brig. Gen. James W. McCauley		
	Col. Clinton C. Wassem	11.7.45	

71st FIGHTER WING

Constituted		11.8.43	
Activated		15.8.43	
Moved to England to join IX FC		12.43	
Returned to USA		11.45 /12.45	
Components:	366th FG		
	368th FG		
	370th FG		
Bases:	Aldermaston	23.12.43	
	Greenham Common	14.1.44	
	Andover	1.3.44	
	Ecrammeville (F)	10.7.44	
	St. Pierre Eglise (F)	1.8.44	
	Ecrammeville (F)	7.8.44	
	Rennes (F)	20.8.44	
	Versailles (F)	9.9.44	
	Vittel (F)	23.10.44	
	Heidelberg (G)	23.4.45	
	Nancy (F)	21.5.45	
	Nancy/Essey (F)	16.7.45	
	Darmstadt (G)	25.9.45	—11.45
Commanding Officers:	Brig. Gen. Ned Schramm		
	2nd Lt. Gordon L. Belsey	9.45	
	Capt. Augustus D. Clemens	26.10.45	—N/K

84th FIGHTER WING

Constituted in USA:		4.11.43	
Activated:		10.11.43	
Moved to England to join IX FC		1.44	
Inactivated		12.8.45	
Components:	50th FG		
	365th FG		
	404th FC		
	405th FG		
Bases:	Keevil	29.1.44	
	Beaulieu	4.3.44	
	Houesville (F)	19.6.44	
	Criqueville (F)	2.8.44	
	Aillieres (F)	30.8.44	
	St. Quentin (F)	12.9.44	
	Vermand (F)	17.9.44	
	Arlon (B)	1.10.44	
	Maastricht (H)	22.10.44	
	Munchen-Gladbach (G)	8.3.45	
	Haltern (G)	3.4.45	
	Gutersloh (G)	14.4.45	
	Braunschweig (G)	22.4.45	—12.8.45
Commanding Officers:	Brig. Gen. Otto P. Weyland		
	Col. Randolph P. Williams	15.2.44	
	Col. Arthur G. Salisbury	8.5.44	
	Col. Dyke F. Meyer	14.9.44	—12.8.45

97th BOMBARDMENT WING

Constituted as 97th Combat BW in USA		2.11.43	
Activated		12.11.43	
Arrived in England to join IX BC from		1.44	
Redesignated 97th CBW(L)		7.44	
Redesignated 97th BW(M)		6.45	
Returned to USA		10.45	
Components:	409th BG		
	410th BG		
	416th BG		
Bases:	Marks Hall	12.11.43	
	Little Walden	13.3.44	
	Voisemon (F)	13.9.44	
	Marchais (F)	13.2.45	
	Arrancy (F)	25.4.45	
	Sandricourt (F)	24.5.45	—1.10.45
Commanding Officers:	Capt. Donald S. Moloney	26.11.43	
	Lt. Col. Chris H. Reuter	2.3.44	
	Brig. Gen. Edward N. Backus	1.4.44	1.10.45

98th BOMBARDMENT WING

Transferred from 8th Air Force as 98th CBW(M)		11.43
Redesignated 98th BW(M)		6.45
Inactivated		27.11.45
Components:	323rd BG	
	387th BG	
	394th BG	
	397th BG	
Bases:	Earls Colne	11.43
	Beaulieu	18.7.44
	Lessay (F)	23.8.44

	Chartres (F)	24.9.44	
	Laon/Athies (F)	3.10.44	
	Havrincourt (F)	1.2.45	
	Venlo (H)	3.3.45	
	Tirlemont (B)	7.45	
	Kitzingen (G)	8.45	
	Namur (B)	10.45	—11.45
Commanding Officers:	Col. Carl R. Storrie	11.43	
	Col. Millard Lewis	21.1.44	
	Brig. Gen. Harold L. Mace	2.8.44	—11.45

99th BOMBARDMENT WING

Transferred from USA as cadre of 99th CBW(M)		11.43	
Redesignated 99th BW(M)		6.45	
Returned to USA		10.45	
Components:	322nd BG (1943-45)		
	344th BG (1943-45)		
	386th BG (1944-45)		
	391st BG (1944-45)		
	394th BG (1945)		
Bases:	Great Dunmow	12.11.43	
	Beaumont (F)	25.9.44	
	Tirlemont (B)	4.45	
	Namur (B)	1.7.45	—9.45
Commanding Officers:	Brig. Gen. Herbert B. Thatcher	12.11.43	
	Col. Reginald F. Vance	7.11.44	
	Maj. Charles F. Salter	1.7.45	
	Lt. Col. William W. Brier	13.7.45	
	Brig. Gen. Richard C. Sanders	12.8.45	—10.45

100th FIGHTER WING

Constituted		8.11.43	
Activated		24.11.43	
Returned to USA		8.45	
Components:	10th PRG		
	48th FG (1944)		
	354th FG (1943-45)		
	358th FG (1944)		
	362nd FG (1944-45)		
	363rd FG (1944)		
	365th FG (1944-45)		
	367th FG (1944-45)		
	368th FG (1944-45)		
	371st FG (1944-45)		
	405th FG (1945)		
	406th FG (1945)		
	474th FG (1944)		
Bases:	Boxted	24.11.43	
	Greenham Common	6.12.43	
	Ibsley	13.1.44	
	Lashenden	15.4.44	
	Criqueville (F)	1.7.44	
	St. Pierre-Eglise(F)	10.7.44	
	Rennes (F)	8.8.44	
	Le Mans (F)	30.8.44	
	St. Dizier (F)	19.9.44	
	Metz (F)	29.12.44	
	Konigstein (G)	14.4.45	—8.45
Commanding Officers:	Col. David B. Lancaster	24.11.43	
	Brig. Gen. Homer L. Sanders	2.1.44	
	Col. Harry B. Young	23.5.45	—8.45

302nd AIR TRANSPORT WING

Contituted		7.44	
Activated		1.9.44	
Transferred to USSTAF		1.9.44	
Returned to 9th Air Force	6.45		
Inactivated		N/K	
Components:	27th ATG (8th AF)		
	31st ATG		
Bases:	Grove	7.44	—1.9.44
	Erding (G)	6.45	—N/K

C-47B 348770 of the 302nd ATW, afterwards a hack at BAD2, Warton   [H. Holmes via D. Benfield]

303rd FIGHTER WING

Constituted in USA		15.11.43	
Activated		24.11.43	
Moved to England to join 9th AF		3.44	
Inactivated		12.8.45	
Components:	36th FG		
	373rd FG		
	406th FG		
Bases:	Ashford	8.3.44	
	La Combe (F)	31.7.44	
	Houesville (F)	2.8.44	
	Rennes (F)	24.8.44	
	Vermand (F)	17.9.44	
	Arlon (B)	3.10.44	
	Maastricht (H)	22.10.44	
	Munchen-Gladbach (G)	8.3.45	
	Haltern (G)	3.4.45	
	Gutersloh (G)	14.4.45	
	Braunschweig (G)	22.4.45	—12.8.45
Commanding Officers:	Brig. Gen. Burton M. Hovey Jr.		
	Col. John R. Ulricson	5.45 —	

CHAPTER 4: THE GROUPS

1st TRANSPORT GROUP (Provisional)

Formed in September 1944 when IX AFSC was given permission to retain up to 48 aircraft for its own transport purposes after the transfer of the 31st ATG to 302nd ATW control, the lst TG (Prov.) originally comprised one ATS and a number of ground units. Twenty-one C-47 and C-53 and ten UC-64 aircraft were assigned at once, and C-46s were added later. Very soon the Group moved to Creil in France and began to carry out its

designated function: providing an air courier service for personnel, the transportation of freight, mail and casualties and ferrying aircraft. For the latter task, a Ferry Squadron was added to the Group. In addition, the Group operated several airstrips in France.

Just after VE-Day, the 31st TG moved into Germany, where it remained until de-activation at the end of 1945.

Squadrons and codes:	315th ATS		
	326th Ferry S (redesignated 325th		
	Ferry S 22.10.45)		
Bases:	Grove	2.9.44	
	Creil (F)	27.9.44	
	Ansbach (G)	22.5.45	-31.12.45
Commanding Officers:	Lt. Col. Harry W. Hopp	2.9.44	—N/K
Aircraft:	C-47; C-53; C-46; UC-64		

3rd COMBAT CREW REPLACEMENT CENTRE GROUP

Although assigned to 8th Air Force Composite Command for administration, 3rd CCRC at Toome in Northern lreland was entirely responsible for the supply of combat-ready crews to the Bombardment Groups of the 9th Air Force. The Group had been formed in August 1943 as the 2902nd HQ and HQ Squadron and the 2905th Replacement and Training Squadron, but these units were redesignated 3rd CCRC Group on 21 November 1943.

The first batch of aircrew arrived from the United States in September 1943, and underwent a three-week course to acclimatise them to UK conditions before being posted as crews to Bombardment Groups in England. As the number of BGs in the

UK increased, so did activity at Toome, and in February 1944 airmen destined to fly A-20s began to arrive. That Spring 3rd CCRC was working at full capacity, but in August new records were set for the number of crews trained — 112 crews for B-26s and 42 for A-20s. During that summer a few instructors at 3rd CCRC took part in operational missions from bases in England to ensure that their teaching methods were effective.

In November 1944 3rd CCRC left Toome to move to Cheddington, but whether much further training was carried out there is uncertain, as the airfield began to be returned to the RAF the following spring.

Bases:	Toome	21.11.43	
	Cheddington	11.44	— N/K
Aircraft:	A-20; B-26		

10th PHOTOGRAPHIC GROUP (later RECONNAISSANCE) GROUP

The 10th PG moved from its training base in the United States to England in January and February 1944 for operations with the 9th Air Force and established its HQ at Chalgrove. There the first of the Group's squadrons, the 30th PRS, was activated on 1 February and assigned to the Group three weeks later. Other squadrons assigned to the Group in its early days in the ETO were the 31st PRS, which joined on 31 March, and 34th PRS, which was assigned two days earlier. These three squadrons

were all based at Chalgrove at this time. The 155th PRS, based at Charmy Down for a short period on arrival in England, was absorbed on 17 May 1944 and moved to Chalgrove three days later.

Up to D-Day, 6 June 1944, the lOth PG was active in photographing a wide variety of strategic targets, including airfields, and a DUC was awarded at the end of May for a particularly useful low-level sortie. Following D-Day, the Group supported the drive across France with day and night photo missions and artillery direction work. Two more squadrons were absorbed on 13 June: 12th TRS and 15th TRS, both from the 67th TRG based at Middle Wallop (although they remained attached to the 67th for the time being), while on the same day the 30th PRS was relinquished to the 67th TRG. The 33rd PRS, which had joined the 10th PG on 1 May, also now transferred to the 67th TRG, but remained on attachment to the 10th until 11 August.

Continuing to follow the Allied armies, the 10th PG took part in the Battle of the Bulge in December 1944/January 1945 and

eventually the crossing of the Rhine. After VE-Day, 8 May 1945, the Group began to break up, the first to go being the 15th TRS, which began the process of returning home in June 1945, the remainder of the Group being retitled the 10th RG that month. The 34th PS, which had been transferred to the 67th TRS on 20 April, returned to the 10th on 11 July and was inactivated in Germany on 22 November 1945, as was the 31st PRS. The 12th TRS and 155th TRS remained in Europe under USAFE control after the inactivation of 9th Air Force.

Code letters 8V indicate the 'ownership' of F-5 267563 by the 31st PS, 10th PG
[Merle Olmsted]

F-6C 2103368 [5M:G] of the 15th TRS, 10th PG, in June 1944; it was probably still attached to the 67th TRG at this time
[via H. Holmes]

Squadrons and codes:	12th TRS [ZM]	(see note A)	
	15th TRS [5M]	(see note B)	
	30th PRS [I6]	(see note C)	
	31st PRS [8V]	(see note D)	
	33rd PRS [SW]	(see note E)	
	34th PRS [S9]	(see note F)	
	155th PRS (formerly 423rd, later 45th)	(see note G)	
Bases (HQ):	Chalgrove	2.44	
	Rennes/St. Jacques (F)	11.8.44	
	Chateaudun (F)	24.8.44	
	St. Dizier (F)	9.44	
	Conflans/Doncourt (F)	11.44	
	Trier/Evren (G)	3.45	
	Ober Olm (G)	5.4.45	
	Furth (G)	28.4.45	—N/K

Bases (Squadrons):

12th TRS:	Middle Wallop	(14.3.44)	
	Le Molay (F)	5.7.44	
	Rennes/St. Jacques (F)	11.8.44	
	Chateaudun (F)	24.8.44	
	St. Dizier (F)	12.9.44	
	Giraumont (F)	30.11.44	
	Euren (G)	29.3.45	
	Ober Olm (G)	2.4.45	
	Furth (G)	28.4.45	—2.12.45
15th TRS:	Middle Wallop	(16.3.44)	
	Chalgrove	27.6.44	
	Rennes/St. Jacques (F)	10.8.44	
	Chateaudun (F)	26.8.44	
	St. Dizier (F)	9.9.44	
	Giraumont (F)	1.12.44	
	Trier/Evren (G)	15.3.45	
	Ober Olm (G)	3.4.45	
	Erfurt (G)	17.4.45	
	Furth (G)	24.4.45	→
30th PRS:	Chalgrove	(1.2.44)	
	Middle Wallop	17.5.44	→
31st PRS:	Chalgrove	(23.3.44)	
	Rennes/St. Jacques (F)	18.8.44	
	Chateaudun (F)	27.8.44	
	St. Dizier (F)	12.9.44	
	Jarny (F)	29.11.44	
	Euren (G)	28.3.45	
	Ober Olm (G)	5.4.45	
	Furth (G)	30.4.45	→
33rd PRS:	Chalgrove	(27.4.44)	
34th PRS:	Chalgrove	(29.3.44)	
	Rennes/St. Jacques (F)	11.8.44	
	Chateaudun (F)	25.8.44	
	St. Dizier (F)	12.9.44	—3.10.44
	Hagenau (G)	(11.7.45)	
	Furth (G)	15.7.45	→
155th PRS:	Charmy Down	(18.4.44)	
	Chalgrove	20.5.44	
	Rennes/St. Jacques (F)	11.8.44	
	Chateaudun (F)	28.8.44	
	St. Dizier (F)	12.9.44	
	Le Culot (B)	13.2.45	—16.2.45
	Furth (G)	24.11.45	—2.12.45
Commanding Officers:	Col. William B. Reed		
	Col. Russell A. Berg	20.6.44	—N/K
Aircraft:	12th TRS: F-6: L-4; P-51; Spitfire		
	15th TRS: F-6: L-4; L-5; P-51; Spitfire		
	30th PRS: F-5; P-38		
	31st PRS: F-5; F-6; P-38; P-51		
	33rd PRS: F-5; P-38; possibly others		
	34th PRS: A-20; F-5; P-38		
	155th PRS: UC-64: F-3: L-4; L-5		

Notes on 10th PG squadrons:

(A) Assigned to 10th PG 13.6.44 but still attached to 67th TRG until 11.8.44

(B) Assigned to 10th PG 13.6.44 but still attached to 67th TRG until 27.6.44

(C) Assigned to 10th PG 21.2.44; to 67th TRG 13.6.44

(D) Assigned to 10th PG 31.3.44 to 22.11.45

(E) Assigned to 10th PG 1.5.44; to 67th TRG 13.6.44 but attached to 10th PG until 11.8.44

(F) Assigned to 10th PG 31.3.44; to XII TAC 3.10.44; reassigned to 10th PG from 69th TRC 11.7.45 to 22.11.45

(G) Assigned to 10th PG 17.5.44; to 67th TRG 21.2.45; reassigned to 10th RG from 64th 24.11.45; active after demise of 9th AF.

Squadron markings:
12th TRS: Yellow spinner and nose band
15th TRS: Blue spinner and nose band

L-4A 215329 coded ZM:3 with vertical tailplane displaying chequerboard markings belonged to the 12th RS of the 10th RG. It was photographed at Furth in Germany in the summer of 1945
[K. Wakefield]

At St. Dizier on 13 September 1944, 15th TRS F-6C 2103433 [5M:H] stands next to the wrecked tailplane of a Luftwaffe aircraft
[via H. Holmes]

31st AIR TRANSPORT GROUP

One of the 9th Air Force's few dedicated transport Groups outside TCC, the 31st ATG was constituted at Camp Griffiths, Bushy Park, on 27 October 1943 and activated the following day, with Col. Carl R. Feldmann as Commanding Officer. The aircraft allocation was to be six single-engined, 20 twin-engined and two four-engined, although it seems doubtful that the latter were ever received. The Group's function was the transportation of passengers, cargo and mail and the ferrying of aircraft, and a number of squadrons were attached for these purposes. Due to an initial shortage of ferry pilots, IX FC supplied them for a time.

On 15 November the 31st ATG moved to Grove, where its first aircraft, named 'Baby Dumpling', was received. By March 1944 the Group was in full swing, serving about twenty airfields on a shuttle basis, and that month 5780 passengers and 400 tons of cargo were carried, 825 aircraft were ferried and 2674 hours were spent in the air. Detachments were sent to Northolt and Harrowbeer in mid-May for mail flying duties.

Just after D-Day, on 11 June 1944, Col. Feldmann flew the Group's first sortie to Normandy to bring back wounded troops, and a week later three officers and sixty enlisted men were flown there to set up and operate a landing strip for cargo and casualty evacuation flights at St. Laurent-sur-Mer, using C-47s and C-53s in which litters had been installed by Grove's two resident MR&R Squadrons.

Following minor reorganisation of the 31st ATG, some confusion was caused by the unofficial status of certain units which had been operating passenger-carrying aircraft on an ad hoc basis. To combine these units into a recognised form, the 302nd ATW was formed in July 1944, and for the time being was placed under the control of the 31st ATG. Very soon, however, the new Wing's HQ was formed and the situation reversed.

To handle the vast amount of freight for France now passing through Grove, a dedicated terminal was set up, able to handle up to twelve aircraft per day. Should this not be adequate, the 31st was able to call upon extra resources from IX AFSC in general. Aircraft of other Commands using Grove were also handled by the 31st ATG. By the end of August 1944, the 31st had evacuated most of the men wounded so far — 26000 — and had carried 6800 tons of cargo from the UK to France.

In August 1944 the Group was alerted for a complete transfer to France, and on 5 September the Group's C-47s and C-53s carried the main party across the Channel. After a move to Chartres in November, the 31st made the return trip, back to Grove, in December 1944 and settled down to operating an intensive service between there and the Continent.

In the early part of 1945 the workload increased to the point where, in March, the Group carried almost a third of the cargo tonnage and over two thirds of the number of evacuated casualties that were carried in the whole of 1944. Cargo tonnage was 8473, evacuees 19151 and other passengers, some from or to a terminal at Biggin Hill, 5187. By that time C-46 aircraft had been added to the Group's fleet, and it was said that 31st ATG aircraft were carrying supplies more expeditiously, and further, than any other means of transport. Among the cargo items were blood plasma, belly tanks for fighter aircraft, chicken wire to stabilise roads, and aviation fuel. Casualty removal included the very first troops airlifted from the east side of the river Rhine.

Ferrying tasks at this time were varied and included the movement of A-26s from UK depots to the Continent.

After 1¾ years under 9th Air Force control, the 31st ATG was transferred to USSAFE on 18 July 1945 and a Unit Citation was awarded in recognition of the Group's efforts.

Squadrons:	313th ATS	
	314th ATS	
	315th ATS	
	316th ATS	
	317th ATS	
	318th ATS	
	319th ATS	
	310th Ferry Sqdn (11.44 - 4.45; ex 27th ATG. 8th AF)	
	325th Ferry Sqdn (12.44 - N/K)	
	326th Ferry Sqdn	
Bases:	Bushy Park (Camp Griffiss)	28.10.43
	Grove	15.11.43
	Querqueville (F)	5.9.44
	Chartres (F)	11.44
	Grove	7.12.44 →
Aircraft:	C-47; C-53; C-46; Oxford; and others	

36th FIGHTER GROUP

36th FG's P-47D 228458 [6V:R] taxies along a PSP strip in Normandy

[H. Holmes]

After a period of service as part of the defence force of the Caribbean area and Panama Canal, the 36th FG returned to the USA in the summer of 1943 to convert to the P-47 aircraft. From its base in Nebraska, the Group moved to England in March and April 1944 and on 8 May began to operate its P-47s on armed reconnaissance, escort and interdiction sorties in preparation for D-Day. During the invasion period, the 36th patrolled the landing zone and flew close-support missions.

In July 1944 the 36th FG moved to France and then assisted during the St. Lo breakthrough and the Third Army offensive. The Group was awarded a DUC in September 1944 for its efforts against enemy forces south of the river Loire. A further move,

into Belgium, took place in October in support of the Ninth Army, and from there the Group took part in the Battle of the Bulge at the end of 1944 and then the First Army's assault on the river Roer in February 1945. In March, operations against the bridge at Remagen were mounted, as were support missions in connection with the airborne crossing of the Rhine. A second DUC was received in April 1945 for sustained attacks on airfields in Bavaria, carried out from captured German bases.

After VE-Day, the 36th FG remained in Germany until being returned, without personnel or equipment, to the USA in February 1946, after the de-activation of the 9th Air Force.

Squadrons and codes:	22nd FS [3T]		
	23rd FS [7U]		
	53rd FS [6V]		
Bases:	Kingsnorth	5.4.44	
	Brucheville (F)	7.7.44	
	Le Mans (F)	23.8.44	
	Athis (F)	23.9.44	
	Juvincourt (F)	1.10.44	
	Le Culot (B)	23.10.44	
	Aachen (G)	28.3.45	
	Neidermennig (G)	8.4.45	
	Kassel/Rothwesten (G)	21.4.45	→
Commanding Officers:	Lt. Col. Van H. Slayden		
	Lt. Col. Paul P. Douglas Jr.	4.45	
	Lt. Col. John L. Wright	30.6.45	
	Maj. Arthur W. Holderness Jr.	25.9.45	
	Lt. Col. William T. McBride	9.11.45	→
Aircraft:	P-47		
Squadron markings:	22nd FS: Red cowling and partial fin and rudder		
	23rd FS: Yellow cowling and partial fin and rudder		
	53rd FS: Blue cowling and partial fin and rudder		

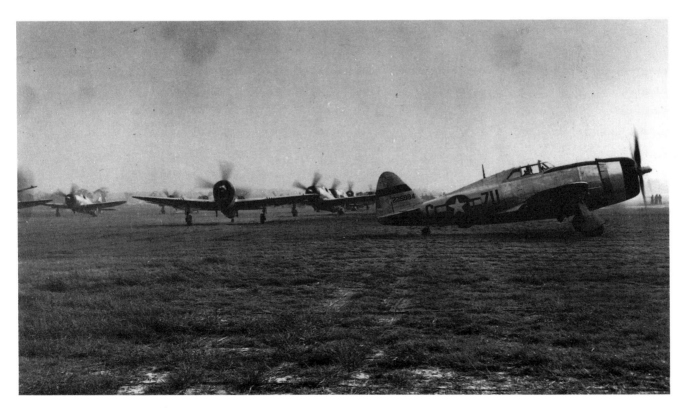

P-47D 225984 [7U:C] of the 36th FG's 23rd FS leads its squadron to the take-off point

[IWM neg. AP22283]

48th FIGHTER GROUP

Originally known as the 48th Fighter-Bomber Group, this Group had operated P-39, P-40 and other aircraft in the USA before being shipped to England in March 1944. Here it converted to P-47s and began operations with a sweep over the French coast on 20 April. The Group was redesignated 48th FG in May 1944.

Escort and dive-bombing sorties were flown by the 48th in advance of the invasion of France, and on D-Day bridges, gun emplacements, trains, road transport and fuel dumps were attacked. With the Allies established in Normandy, the 48th FG moved there on 18 June and then supported the drive across France to take part in the Allied attack on Holland in Sep-

tember. A move was made to Belgium at the end of September, and two Belgian citations were received in recognition of the Group's activities that autumn. A further reward came in December in the shape of a DUC for facing intense opposition from an enemy stronghold. The 48th took part in the Battle of the Bulge in December 1944/January 1945 and continued tactical operations until VE-Day, added to which weather reconnaissance flights were made and on one occasion blood plasma was dropped in belly tanks to troops below.

The 48th Fighter Group returned to the USA in August and September 1945.

Squadrons and codes:	492nd FS [F4]		
	493rd FS [I7]		
	494th FS [6M]		
Bases:	Ibsley	29.3.44	
	Deux Jumeaux (F)	18.6.44	
	Villacoublay (F)	29.8.44	
	Cambrai/Niergnies (F)	15.9.44	
	St. Trond (B)	30.9.44	
	Kelz (G)	26.3.45	
	Kassel (G)	17.4.45	
	Illesheim (G)	29.4.45	
	Laon (F)	5.7.45	—8.45
Commanding Officers:	Col. Dixon M. Allison		
	Col. George L. Wertenbaker Jr.	23.4.44	
	Col. James K. Johnson	10.44	
	Lt. Col. Harold L. McNeely	8.6.45	
	Lt. Col. Paul P. Douglas Jr.	28.6.45	
Aircraft:	P-47		
Squadron markings:	492nd FS: Red rudder and front of cowling		
	493rd FS: Blue rudder and front of cowling		
	494th FS: Yellow rudder and front of cowling		
	All with red and white chequered cowling		

50th FIGHTER GROUP

Tasked in the USA with the operational training of pilots, using P-40s, P-47s, P-51s and other types, the 50th FG moved to England in March and April 1944 to concentrate on P-47s. An initial fighter sweep was made over the French coast on 1 May, after which dive-bombing and escort missions occupied the Group until D-Day, when it concentrated on covering the landings.

On D+19 the 50th FG moved to France and made concentrated attacks on tactical targets, following the Allied

advance across France, and came under the control of 1st Tactical Air Force on 1 November 1944. In January 1945 the Group began to take part in the drive which resulted in the Allied entry into southern Germany, and in March was awarded a DUC for its close cooperation with the Seventh Army's assault on the Siegfried Line. Another DUC arrived after an attack on an airfield near Munich on 25 April.

After VE-Day, the 50th FG remained in Germany until August 1945, when it returned to the United States.

Squadrons and codes:	10th FS [T5]		
	81st FS [2N]		
	313th FS [W3]		
Bases:	Lymington	5.4.44	
	Carentan (F)	25.6.44	
	Meautis (F)	16.8.44	
	Paris/Orly (F)	4.9.44	
	Laon (F)	15.9.44	
	Lyon/Bron (F)	28.9.44	
	Toul/Croix de Metz (F)	3.11.44	
	Giebelstadt (G)	20.4.45	
	Mannheim (G)	21.5.45	—22.6.45
Commanding Officers:	Col. William D. Greenfield		
	Col. Harvey L. Case Jr.	11.44	—8.45

Aircraft: P-47

Squadron markings: Coloured nose band and horizontal stripes across all three tailplane surfaces

P-47D 225904 [2N:U] sitting on Carentan airstrip in close proximity to some of the original inhabitants. Note the crashed RAF Spitfire in the background

[IWM neg. EA28806]

61st TROOP CARRIER GROUP

Code 3I identifies this C-47 as belonging to the 61st TCG's 14th TCS; note Donald Duck nose-art   [R. Mynn]

Well experienced in troop carrying operations with the 12th Air Force in the Mediterranean area, the 61st TCG arrived at Barkston Heath in England from Sicily in February 1944 to join IX TCC in preparation for the invasion of Europe. As this airfield was not quite ready for use, training was limited for a time, but soon the momentum increased and the 61st became very busy.

Just before midnight on 5/6 June 1944, the 61st's C-47s began to get airborne with their loads of paratroopers of the 507th Paratroop Infantry Regiment. 72 aircraft took part, dropping the paratroops near St. Mere Eglise, after which the C-47s returned to base at dawn. One aircraft was shot down and several others damaged, including that of the CO, Col. Mitchell. Resupply missions by 52 aircraft were carried out next morning, but this time three aircraft were so severely damaged that they were forced to ditch in the English Channel.

Further training exercises followed, in order to prepare the Group for participation in Operation Market Garden, the assault on Arnhem. On 17 September 1944 72 aircraft left Barkston Heath carrying British paratroops, and next day 123 CG-4 gliders were towed to the Arnhem area carrying reinforcements.

The 61st TCG moved to France in March 1945 to take part in the airborne crossing of the Rhine, when it again dropped British troops. Subsequently, the 61st became a transport unit, carrying food, fuel and other supplies and evacuating the wounded. In May 1945, its task complete, the 61st TCG moved to Trinidad.

Squadrons and codes:	14th TCS [31]		
	15th TCS [Y9]		
	53rd TCS [3A]		
	59th TCS [X5]		
Bases:	Barkston Heath	18.2.44	
	Abbeville (F)	13.3.45	−19.5.45
Commanding Officers:	Col. Willis W. Mitchell		
	Col. Edgar W. Hampton	12.4.45	−N/K
Aircraft:	C-47; C-109; CG-4		

British paratroops about to board a 61st TCG C-47 at Barkston Heath in September 1944   [D. Benfield]

Waco CG-4 gliders massed at Barkston Heath in 1944; C-47 tugs are seen in the background   [D. Benfield]

67th TACTICAL RECONNAISSANCE GROUP

Originally assigned to the 8th Air Force in the United Kingdom, the 67th Reconnaisance Group, comprising at the time the 12th TRS, 107th TRS, 109th TRS and 153rd LS, transferred to the 9th Air Force in October 1943. Having trained for over a year, the Group began operations in December 1943, using mainly P-38s, P-51s and F-5s on artillery-adjustment, photo-reconnaissance, weather-reconnaissance and raid assessment sorties. During December, the 153rd LS left the Group to become an independent sqaudron but early in January 1944 the 15th TRS joined the Group.

During the run-up to the invasion of Europe, the 67th, now a TRG, carried out difficult low-level photographic sorties along the French coast and then used all its expertise in support of the landings on 6 June. Two squadrons, the 12th and 15th, were transferred to the 10th PRG on 13 June, and the 30th PRS joined the Group. The first of the 67th's squadrons to cross the English Channel to an ALG was the 107th, which found its new home at Deux Jumeaux on 28 June, and the other squadrons had moved to France by mid-August.

Following the invasion, the 67th gave its support to the Allied advance across France and was active over the Siegfried Line between September and December 1944 and in the Ardennes during the Battle of the Bulge in December 1944 and January 1945. Finally the Group assisted the Allied crossing of the Rhine and into Germany.

After VE-Day, the 67th TRG was redesignated as the 67th RG in June 1945, and the gradual winding-down process began. The 33rd PRS was transferred to the 363rd RG on 5 July, while the 30th PRS, 107th TRS and 109th TRS all began the lengthy process of returning to the USA in July 1945.

Squadrons and codes:	12th TRS [ZM]	(see note A)
	15th TRS	(see note B)
	30th PRS [I6]	(see note C)
	33rd PRS [SW]	(see note D)
	107th TRS [AX]	(see note E)
	109th TRS [VX]	(see note E)
	153rd LS [ZS]	(see note F)

Notes on 67th TRG squadrons:
(A) Assigned to 67th TRC from 29.3.42; transferred to 10th PG 13.6.44 but remained attached to 67th TRG until 11.8.44
(B) Assigned to 67th TRG from 4.1.44; transferred to 10th PG 13.6.44 but remained attached to 67th TRG until 27.6.44, and one Flight was further attached from 3.8.44 to 12.8.44
(C) Assigned to 67th TRG from 13.6.44 upon transfer from 10th PG: operated from Florennes (B) 8.12.44 to 18.12.44; assigned elsewhere 7.45
(D) Assigned to 67th TRG from 13.6.44 upon transfer from 10th PG; reassigned to XXIX TAC (Prov.) 7.10.44 but remained attached to 67th TRG until 2.11.44, after reassignment to 363rd TRG on 30.10.44; further assignment to 67th TRG, later RG, from 17.5.45 to 5.7.45
(E) Operated from Chievres from 7.12.44 to 18.12.44
(F) Became an independent squadron on 12.12.43

Squadron markings:
12th TRS: Yellow spinner and nose band
15th TRS: Blue spinner and nose band

F-6B 2103622 [AX:G] of the 107th TRS, 67th TRG   [Merle Olmsted]

Bases (HQ):	Membury	(10.42)	
	Middle Wallop	12.43	
	Le Molay (F)	7.44	
	Toussus le Noble (F)	8.44	
	Gosselies (B)	9.44	
	Vogelsang (G)	3.45	
	Limburg an der Lahn (G)	2.4.45	
	Eschwege (G)	10.4.45	—7.45
Bases (Squadrons):			
12th TRS:	Greenham Common	16.12.43	
	Aldermaston	9.1.44	
	Chilbolton	1.3.44	
	Middle Wallop	14.3.44	
	Le Molay (F)	5.7.44	—11.8.44
15th TRS:	Aldermaston	22.12.43	
	Chilbolton	1.3.44	
	Middle Wallop	16.3.44	—27.6.44
30th PRS:	Middle Wallop	17.5.44	
	Le Molay (F)	3.7.44	
	Toussus-le-Noble (F)	31.8.44	
	Gosselies (B)	22.9.44	
	Vogelsang (G)	24.3.45	
	Limburg an der Lahn (G)	2.4.45	
	Eschwege (G)	10.4.45	—7.45
33rd PRS:	Chalgrove	27.4.44	
	Le Molay (F)	15.8.44	
	Toussus-le-Noble (F)	30.8.44	
	Gosselies (B)	21.9.44	—5.11.44
	Eschwege (G)	17.5.45	—5.7.45
107th TRS:	Membury	(8.1.43)	
	Middle Wallop	11.12.43	
	Deux Jumeaux (F)	28. 6.44	
	Le Molay (F)	5.7.44	
	Toussus-le-Noble (F)	29.8.44	
	Gosselies (B)	16.9.44	
	Vogelsang (G)	23.3.45	
	Limburg an der Lahn (G)	4.4.45	
	Eschwege (G)	9.4.45	—5.7.45
109th TRS:	Membury	(15.5.43)	
	Middle Wallop	12.12.43	
	Le Molay (F)	4.7.44	
	Toussus-le-Noble (F)	29.8.44	
	Buc (F)	31.8.44	
	Gosselies (B)	20.9.44	
	Vogelsang (G)	23.3.45	
	Limburg an der Lahn (G)	4.4.45	
	Echwege (G)	9.4.45	—5.7.45
153rd LS:	Membury	(3.10.43)	
	Keevil	28.11.43	—12.12.43
Commanding Officers:	Col. Frederick R. Anderson		
	Col. George W. Peck	6.12.43	
	Lt. Col. Richard S. Leghorn	11.5.45-	—N/K

Aircraft:	12th TRS:	Spitfire; F-6; P-51
	15th TRS:	Spitfire; F-6; L-4; L-5; P-51
	30th PRS:	F-5; P-38
	33rd PRS:	F-5; P-38; P-51; possibly others
	107th TRS:	Spitfire; F-6; P-51
	109th TRS:	Spitfire; F-6; L-4; P-51
	153rd LS:	A-20; L-4; possibly others

69th TACTICAL RECONNAISSANCE GROUP

Training with F-6 and A-26 aircraft by the 69th TRG began in the United States in January 1945, and a move was made in March to France to join the 9th Air Force, absorbing in the process the Provisional Reconnaissance Group's three squadrons. After settling down, the 69th flew photographic and visual missions until VE-Day, and was redesignated as the 69th RG in June before all but the 10th RS returned home in July and August 1945.

Squadrons and codes:	10th TRS [YC]		
	22nd TRS [QL]		
	34th PRS [XX]		
	111th TRS [N5]		
Bases:	Nancy (F)	22.3.45	
	Haguenau (F)	2.4.45	— 30.6.45
Commanding Officers:	Col. John T. Shields		
Aircraft:	10th TRS: A-24; B-25; F-6; L-5; P-40; P-51		
	22nd TRS: F-6: P-40; P-51		
	34th PRS: A-20; F-5; P-38		
	111th TRS: F-6; L-5; P-51; UC-64		

Squadron markings:
10th TRS: Red fin and rudder (quartered)
22nd TRS: Green fin and rudder (quartered)
34th PRS: N/K
111th TRS: coloured fin and rudder

313th TROOP CARRIER GROUP

The 313th TCG's HQ and one squadron transferred from the 12th Air Force in Sicily to join IX TCC at Folkingham on 4 February 1944, the Group's other three squadrons following early in March. Training for the invasion of Europe then proceeded, until on D-Day the Group's seventy C-47 and C-53 aircraft arrived over the DZ near Picauville with troops of the 82nd Airborne Division. During this mass drop the Group lost three aircraft, but next day 52 aircraft took off on a vital re-supply mission. For its efforts, the 313th TCG was awarded a DUC.

Training then resumed, and continued until on 17 September 1944 the 313th was once again active, ninety aircraft carrying British paratroops to the Arnhem area. Next day, and on 23 September, 180 gliders were towed by the 313th to the same area, carrying much-needed supplies and reinforcements. After the Arnhem operation, the 313th gathered that its 29th TCS was to become a C-87 unit, assigned to tow the heavy CG-13A glider, which the C-47 was unable to do. Late in 1944 a B-24 arrived at Folkingham to enable training to begin, followed a few days later by a C-109. When the crews found out that they would be carrying fuel and not towing gliders the enthusiasm evaporated.

The single C-109 remained with the 29th TCS until the end of hostilities.

In January 1945 a CG-13A glider arrived at Folkingham and a gradual conversion to the C-46 began. While this took place, general transportation and casualty evacuation duties were maintained until in February and March a move to France was made so that the Group could take part in the airborne crossing of the Rhine. More paratroops were carried on 24 March, this time those of the 17th Airborne Division, who dropped near Wesel.

The 313th TCG's final operation of note took place on 10 May 1945, two days after VE Day, when some of the C-46s were positioned at Barkston Heath for a trip to Stavanger in Norway. From Barkston they carried British troops who set up a mobile air traffic control unit on Stavanger/Sola airfield under the eyes of Luftwaffe personnel who had not been disarmed. During the next few days the 313th carried members of the British 1st Airborne Division to form the main party of liberation. In August 1945 the 313th TCG, its duties complete, returned to the USA.

Squadrons and codes:	29th TCS [5X]		
	47th TCS [N3]		
	48th TCS [Z7]		
	49th TCS [H2]		
Bases:	Folkingham	4.2.44	
	Achiet (F)	26.2.45	—5.8.45
Commanding Officers:	Col. James J. Roberts Jr.		
	Lt. Col. William A. Filer	18.3.45	
	Lt. Col. Paul W. Stephens	26.3.45	—5.8.45
Aircraft:	C-47; C-53; C-46; CG-4.		

This slightly censored picture shows a 5X-coded C-46 of the 48th TCS, 313rd TCG, at Achiet, France in March 1945   [via D. Benfield]

One of the rare CG-13 gliders as used by the 313th TCG at Folkingham   (Blickenderfer via D. Benfield)

C-46D 477540 [H2:L] was the first example of the type received by the 313th TCG [Blickenderfer via D. Benfield]

This B-24J, 440121, was used by the 313th TCG for training crews to operate the C-109 fuel tanker conversion [Blickenderfer via D. Benfield]

314th TROOP CARRIER GROUP

Another Troop Carrier Group which transferred from the 12th Air Force in the Mediterranean area was the 314th TCG, which arrived in England in February 1944 to train for the forthcoming invasion of Europe. Paratroops were dropped from the Group's 51 C-47s and nine C-53s near Renville on D-Day and resupply missions were flown in poor weather on subsequent days, earning the Group a DUC.

When the Allied forces had become established in Normandy, the 314th flew supply sorties to the beach-head area until September 1944, when the Group played its part in the Arnhem operation. On 17 and 18 September the 314th's C-47s and C-53s carried paratroops and equipment, losing four aircraft to enemy gunfire in the process. The Group then reverted to general supply and casualty evacuation missions until being called upon for the third time, this time to take part in Operation Varsity, the airborne crossing of the Rhine in March 1945. This comprised, for the 314th, the task of towing eighty CG-4 gliders from the Group's base at Poix in France, to which it had moved recently, to the Wesel area.

The Group then carried out transport missions until VE-Day, when it began to evacuate Allied prisoners of war from Germany. Scheduled flights within Europe were then the main task of the 314th TCC, which became part of USAFE on the deactivation of the 9th Air Force in December 1945.

Squadrons and codes:	32nd TCS [S2]			
	50th TCS [2R]			
	61st TCS [Q9]			
	62nd TCS [E5]			
Bases:	32nd TCS:	Saltby	20.2.44	
		Poix (F)	28.2.45	
		Frankfurt (G) (see note 1)	23.9.45	→
	50th TCS:	Saltby	6.3.44	
		Poix (F)	5.3.45	→
	61st TCS:	Saltby	24.2.44	
		Poix (F)	2.45	
		Frankfurt (G) (see note 2)	15.10.45	→
	62nd TCS:	Saltby	25.2.44	
		Poix (F)	3.45	
		Villacoublay (F)	15.10.45	→
Commanding Officers:	Col. Clayton Stiles			
	Lt. Col. Halac G. Wilson		22.8.45	
	Col. Charles W. Steinmetz		29.11.45	→
Aircraft:	C-47; C-53; CG-4; Horsa			

Notes: 1. attached to 441st TCG 9.45 and assigned 12.45 On.
2. attached to 441st TCG 10.45 and assigned 12.45 on.

The Ninth Air Force also used examples of the British-made Horsa glider; this one still bears RAF roundels [via D. Benfield]

A line-up of C-47s of the 32nd TCS, 314th TCG, ready to take off from Saltby in September 1944 for Operation Market Garden [D. Benfield]

After an earlier period of service in England with the 8th Air Force, the 315th TCG moved to Algeria in May 1943 to join the 12th Air Force. In November of that year Group HQ returned to England to become part of IX TCC at Welford, leaving the two squadrons, the 34th and the 43rd, at Blida, but in February 1944 all three units came together at Spanhoe. There, in April, they were joined by two more squadrons which had arrived direct from the United States. The entire Group then got down to the task of training for D-Day. Early on 6 June 1944 the 315th TCG's C-47s and C-53s dropped paratroops of the 82nd Airborne Division at St. Mere Eglise as their contribution to Operation Neptune, later receiving a DUC for this and subsequent re-supply missions carried out by the Group. After D-Day, training continued in view of the probability of further airborne operations as the assault on Europe developed. It was while the assembly of a formation was taking place on 8 July for a practice drop on Wittering airfield that two of the Group's C-47s collided, both crashing near Ketton in Rutland. Eight crew members and 26 paratroops died in this unfortunate incident, but there were a few survivors. Then came Operation Market Garden, the assault on Arnhem, and on 17 September 1944 the 315th TCG dropped men of the 82nd Airborne Division, following this mission with reinforcement sorties. General transport work was carried out for the next few months, and to enable liquid fuel to be carried, four C-109s (converted B-24s) joined the Group in December 1944. The final task for the 315th TCG in Europe came in March 1945, when it took part in Operation Varsity, the crossing of the river Rhine. This time the troops carried were those of the British Sixth Airborne Division, who were uplifted from Boreham. Casualty evacuation work followed, continuing after the Group moved to France in April 1945. Its stay there was short, as it was re-assigned to Trinidad in May 1945.

The 315th TCG's C-47A 315253 [4A:F] in the snow at Spanhoe during the winter of 1944/45   [via D. Benfield]

Warhorses of the 315th TCG's 309th TCS
[via D. Benfield]

Squadrons and codes:	34th TCS [NM]		
	43rd TCS [UA]		
	309th TCS [M6]		
	310th TCS [4A]		
Bases:	Welford (HQ)	6.11.43	
	Spanhoe (HQ and two squadrons)	7.2.44	
	Spanhoe (complete Group)	21.4.44	
	Amiens (F)	6.4.45	—5.45
Commanding Officers:	Col. Hamish McLelland		
	Col. Howard B. Lyon	27.9.44	
	Lt. Col. Robert J. Gibbons	27.3.45	—5.45
Aircraft:	C-47; C-53; C-109; Oxford (3); L-4 (3); CG-4; Horsa		

This picture shows the modifications carried out on the noses of B-24s converted to C-109 tankers; this example belongs to the 315th TCG [via D. Benfield]

This C-109 is not idenitified, but the code 4A carried by the C-47 behind it signifies the 315th TCG

[D. Benfield]

In February 1944 the 316th TCG, released from operating in Italy, moved to England to join the 9th Air Force and to train for the invasion of Europe. On D-Day the Group's 72 C-47s and C-53s dropped paratroops at St. Mere Eglise and followed this next day and subsequently with supply missions. Next the 316th took part in the attacks on Holland in September 1944 by towing 171 CG-4 gliders carrying troops, and in the river Rhine crossing offensive in March 1945, for which the Group's aircraft used Wethersfield as a jumping off point.

Before leaving for home in May 1945 the 316th TCG continued to mount supply and casualty evacuation missions.

Squadrons and codes:	36th TCS [6E]		
	37th TCS [W7]		
	44th TCS [4C]		
	45th TCS [T3]		
Bases:	Cottesmore	15.2.44	−5.45
Commanding Officers:	Lt. Col. Burton R. Fleet*		−12.5.44
	Col. Harvey A. Berger	13.5.44	−N/K
	*killed in flying accident 11/12.5.44		
	during Exercise Eagle		
Aircraft:	C-47; C-53; C-46; CG-4		

C-46D 477819 [4C:Y] of the 44th TCS, 316th TCG, seen with another C-46 and two C-109s in the background, at Cottesmore [W. Ferguson, via N. Roberson]

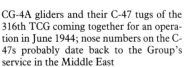

CG-4A gliders and their C-47 tugs of the 316th TCG coming together for an operation in June 1944; nose numbers on the C-47s probably date back to the Group's service in the Middle East
[via D. Benfield]

C-47s of the 316th TCG at Cottesmore in 1944; note CG-4As being towed off in the background   [W. Ferguson via N. J. Robertson]

322nd BOMBARDMENT GROUP

One of the four original constituent Groups of the 9th Air Force in England, the 322nd BG had been assigned to the 8th Air Force on arrival in December 1942. Operations had commenced in May 1943, when twelve of the Group's B-26s had carried out very low-level attacks on a power station in Holland.

The main targets raided by the 322nd from July 1943 through October, when the Group transferred to the 9th Air Force, to February 1944, were airfields in France, Belgium and Holland, although power stations, railway yards, construction sites and other strategic targets were not overlooked. In March 1944 the Group began to take part in the overall softening-up process prior to the invasion of Europe. Road and railway bridges,

coastal gun batteries, oil tank farms and V.1 sites were now given priority attention.

After D-Day, the 322nd followed the Third Army's drive across France, moving there in September to be nearer the action. In the late autumn of 1944 the 322nd took part in the assault on the Siegfried Line and then was involved in the Battle of the Bulge until early January 1945. The Group then concentrated on finishing off enemy resistance, moving to Belgium in March 1945, before flying a final mission on 24 April. In June 1945 the 322nd moved into Germany, where it was employed in dismantling Luftwaffe equipment, before returning home to the USA in November and December 1945 to be inactivated.

Squadrons and codes:	449th BS [PN]	**Group marking:** light coloured rudder.		
	450th BS [ER]			
	451st BS [SS]			
	452nd BS [DR]			
Bases:	Andrews Field		12.6.43	
	Beauvais/Tille (F)		25.9.44	
	Le Culot (B)		30.3.45	
	Fritzlar (G)		6.45*	
	Clastres (F)		10.45	—11.45
*449th BS at Honau/Langendiebach (G)		7.45—9.45		
450th BS at Frankenburg (G)		7.45—9.45, Arolsen (G) 9.45—10.45		
451st BS at Arolsen (G)		7.45—10.45		
452nd BS at Wickenrode (G)		6.45—7.45, Hornel (G) 7.45— 10.45		
Commanding Officers:	Col. Glenn C. Nye			
	Col. John S. Samuel		6.44	
	Maj. John L. Egan		12.7.45	— N/K
Aircraft:	B-26			

131788 is a B-26B, while 134763 [PN:A] is a B-26C; both are from the 322nd BG's 449th BS, based at Andrews Field

323rd BOMBARDMENT GROUP

Originally based at Horham with the 8th Air Force, the 323rd BG became one of the original 9th Air Force Groups on 16 October 1943, by which time a move to Earls Colne had been made. Operations against strategic targets in France, Holland and Belgium had been started in June 1943 and continued after the re-assignment. Additional targets early in 1944 were V.1 sites in the Pas de Calais and, at the end of February, concerted attacks on airfields in Holland were made by the Group's B-26s.

Leading up to the invasion of Normandy and on D-Day itself, the 323rd concentrated its efforts against road and rail communications and subsequently took part in the July breakthrough at St Lo. A move to France was made in August 1944, and soon afterward the Group flew its first night mission, an attack on gun batteries near St. Malo; for this purpose the aircraft were repainted black.

Early in September 1944 the 323rd wiped out a number of strong points at Brest before moving its area of operation to eastern France to support the attack on the Siegfried Line. The Group was highly effective in knocking out enemy transport bringing reinforcements to the Ardennes during the Christmas 1944 counter-offensive, for which efforts a DUC was received. Thereafter, the 323rd supported the advance through Germany to complete its offensive activities in April 1945. After VE-Day, the 323rd BG participated in the disarmament programme until returning to the USA in December 1945.

Squadrons and codes:	453rd BS [VT]	Group marking: white horizontal stripe (edged black on aircraft with nat-	
	454th BS [RJ]	ural metal finish) across fin and	
	455th BS [YU]	rudder	
	456th BS [WT]		
Bases:	Earls Colne		
	Beaulieu	21.7.44	
	Lessay (F)	26.8.44	
	Chartres (F)	21.9.44	
	Laon/Athies (F)	13.10.44	
	Denain/Prouvy (F)	9.2.45	
	Gablingen (G)	15.5.45	
	Landsberg (G) (HQ only)*	16.7.45	
	Clastres (F)	10.45—	
		12.45	
Note: Squadrons were detached as follows:			
	453rd BS Augsburg (G)	15.5.45	
	Haunstetten (G)	12.7.45	−10.45
	454th BS Valenciennes (F)	9.2.45	
	Innsbruck (A)	15.5.45	
	Nesselwang (G)	9.7.45	
	Schongrau (G)	7.45	−10.45
	455th BS Leipheim (G)	23.5.45	−10.45
	456th BS Kempten (G)	20.5.45	−10.45
Commanding Officers:	Col. Herbert B. Thatcher		
	Col. Wilson R. Wood	13.11.43	
	Col. Rollin M. Winingham	14.2.45	
	Lt. Col. George O. Commenator	8.45	−N/K
Aircraft:	B-26		

A 456th BS B-26 about to receive attention at the vast BAD1, Burtonwood, in 1944 [Carl J. Winkleman via Aldon Ferguson]

344th BOMBARDMENT GROUP

After a period of service as a replacement training unit, the 344th moved to England in January and February 1944 and began operations on 6 March. For the first two months a wide variety of strategic targets was attacked, and then from May the Group assisted in the softening-up of the French coastal region in readiness for the invasion. On D-Day the 344th attacked coastal gun batteries at Cherbourg and subsequently supported the armies' drive through the Cotentin peninsula and bombed defensive positions near Caen to assist the British efforts.

The 344th received a DUC for a three-day assault on troop

build-ups, supply dumps, roads and railway bridges near St. Lo at the end of June 1944 and then attacked shipping at Brest. Strategic targets in Germany then became the object of the Group's attention until the end of April 1945.

Following the end of hostilities in Europe, the 344th BG was involved in training and demonstration flights in Germany, to where the Group moved in September 1945, eventually severing its connection with the 9th Air Force when the latter disbanded in December 1945.

Squadrons and codes:	494th BS [K9]	Group marking: white triangle
	495th BS [Y5]	on fin and rudder
	496th BS [N3]	
	497th BS [7I]	
Bases:	Stansted	9.2.44
	Cormeilles-en-Vexin (F)	30.9.44
	Florrenes/Juzaine (B)	5.4.45
	Schleissheim (G)	15.9.45 →
Commanding Officers:	Col. Reginald F. Vance	19.9.43
	Col. Robert W. Witty	7.11.44
	Lt. Col. Lucius D. Clay Jr.	18.8.45 →
Aircraft:	B-26	

349th TROOP CARRIER GROUP

An unusual 9th Air Force Group in that it hardly saw any active service in the ETO, the 349th TCG did not arrive in England from the USA until the end of March 1945. This was too late to take part in any of the important troop-carrying operations, but the 349th quickly settled down to the task of delivering supplies of all sorts to continental Europe, including liquid fuel, for which the Group used two C-109s. Flying the uncommon C-46 aircraft, the 349th TCG also evacuated wounded troops and prisoners of war.

Hardly had the 349th settled down at Barkston Heath when in mid-April it moved to France. A few aircraft returned to Barkston Heath, and to Saltby, early in May, however, to airlift British airborne troops to Norway, but the 349th's detachment returned to France after about two weeks.

The 349th TCG was inactivated in July 1945 and by August the men and equipment had begun the journey back to the United States.

Squadrons and codes:	23rd TCS [Q8]		
	312th TCS [9E]		
	313th TCS [3F]		
	314th TCS		
Bases:	Barkston Heath	30.3.45	
	Roye/Amy (F)	18.4.45	—13.7.45
Commanding Officers:	Col. Leonard J. Barrow Jr.		
Aircraft:	C-46 (64); C-109 (2)		

354th FIGHTER GROUP

The first Fighter Group to be equipped with the P-51B, the 354th moved to England to join the newly-constituted 9th Air Force in October and November 1943. The Group then carried out the 9th Air Force's first P-51B mission, a Rodeo over northern France, on 5 December. Subsequently, the 354th was involved in the development and practice of long-range escort missions with the 8th Air Force 'heavies' on raids deep inside enemy territory, an activity for which a DUC was awarded in May 1944. By the end of that month, the 354th had carried out 93 missions and claimed 324 enemy aircraft destroyed and 39 probably so, for the loss of 67 of its P-51s and 63 pilots.

The 354th FG then began fighter-bomber operations against enemy airfields, roads, railways and supply dumps in France, Belgium and Holland. On D-Day, 6 June 1944, the Group escorted the glider 'trains' and then set about wiping out strategic targets near the front line. Shortly afterwards, after carrying out some anti-V.1 'Diver' sorties over Kent, the Group moved from its ALG in England to France, and subsequently supported the Allied advance. A second DUC was received by the 354th for its fighter sweeps on 25 August 1944, when Group aircraft battled with 25 or more Fw190s in the Reims area, shooting down ten of them and destroying several on the ground. In September the 354th supported the airborne assault on Holland, and later took part in the attack on the Siegfried Line by destroying enemy transportation and troops. A part was also played in the Battle of the Bulge around Christmas 1944, when the Group operated from St. Dizier. Finally, the 354th FG helped ground forces in the crossing of the Rhine.

After VE-Day, the 354th FG remained in Germany up to and beyond the disbandment of the 9th Air Force.

Ground crew men work on repairs to P-51B 463562 [GQ:H] of the 354th FG in the ruins of a hangar at Ober Olm, Germany, on 17 April 1945

[via H. Holmes]

Squadrons and codes:	353rd FS [FT]	
	355th FS [GQ]	
	356th FS [AJ]	
Bases:	Greenham Common	4.11.43
	Boxted	13.11.43
	Lashenden	17.4.44
	Criqueville (F)	17.6.44
	Gael (F)	14.8.44
	Orconte (F)	21.9.44
	Rosieres-en-Haye (F)*	1.12.44
	Ober Olm (G)	7.4.45
	Ansbach (G)	1.5.45
	Herzogenaurach (G)	15.4.45

*HQ at Meurthe-et-Moselle

Commanding Officers:	Col. Kenneth R. Martin		
	Col. James R. Howard	12.2.44	
	Col. George R. Bickell	4.44	
	Lt. Col. Jack T. Bradley	5.45	—N/K
Aircraft:	P-51 (11.43—11.44, 2.45 →)		
	P-47 (11.44—2.45)		

Squadron markings:

353rd FS P-51s:	Yellow/white nose bands; later yellow spinner and nose
P-47s:	Yellow cowling
355th FS P-51s:	Blue spinner and nose tip
P-47s:	Light blue nose band and chequered cowling, black horizontal band across fin and rudder
356th FS P-51s:	Red spinner and nose band; black horizontal band across fin and rudder
P-47s:	Red cowling

Named 'Ensign Babs' and coded GQ:I is this P-51 463668, of the 354th FG
[Merle Olmsted]

Auxiliary fuel tanks being fitted to P-51 'Peggy' of the 355th FS, 354th FG, probably at Boxted, in the winter of 1943/44
[via H. Holmes]

Battle-stained P-51B 'Little Chris II' of the 353rd FS, 354th FG, at Lashenden ALG being inspected by ground crew men [via H. Holmes]

357th FIGHTER GROUP

The second Group in the 9th Air Force to receive P-51s, the 357th FG arrived at Raydon from the USA in November 1943, but the urgent need of the 8th Air Force saw the Group transferred to the 8th in late January 1944, before becoming combat-ready.

Squadrons and codes:	362nd FS [G4]		
	363rd FS [B6]		
	364th FS [C5]		
Bases:	Raydon	30.11.43	—31.1.44
Commanding Officer:	Col. Henry R. Spicer		
Aircraft:	P-51		
Squadron markings:	362nd FS: (none)		
	363rd FS: Red rudder		
	364th FS: Yellow rudder		

358th FIGHTER GROUP

Its period of training in the USA completed, the 358th FG was shipped to England in October 1943 to join the 8th Air Force, but was transferred to the 9th on 1 February 1944. For a time, the Group was involved in escorting heavy bombers of the 8th Air Force, but on moving to an ALG in the south of England in April 1944 a switch to the fighter-bomber role was made so that the Group could concentrate on attacks on marshalling yards and airfields in France. This was the routine until D-Day, when the 358th escorted C-47s over the Cotentin peninsula, after which a reversion to the fighter-bomber role was made.

In July 1944 the 358th moved to France, and continued to fly escort and close-support missions before transferring to 1st TAF control on 15 November 1944. The Group earned a DUC for the efforts it made during the period 24 December 1944 to 2 January 1945, when, operating from St. Dizier, it not only gave vital support to the US 7th Army but wiped out many Luftwaffe aircraft during their assault on Allied airfields. A second DUC was received for operations in March 1945 during the German withdrawal across the Rhine. Yet another DUC was awarded to the 358th FG in recognition of its efforts during the final month of the war, when concerted attacks were made on airfields in Bavaria and on the few remaining strategic targets.

With victory in Europe declared, the 358th FG was able to return to the USA in July 1945 to be inactivated later that year.

Squadrons and codes:	365th FS [CH]		
	366th FS [IA]		
	367th FS [CP]		
Commanding Officers:	Col. Cecil L. Wells		
	Col. James B. Tipton	20.9.44	
	Lt. Col. John M. Thacker	45	—N/K
Bases:	Raydon	31.1.44	
	High Halden	13.4.44	
	Cretteville (F)	3.7.44	
	Pontorson (F)	14.8.44	
	Vitry-le-Francois (F)	15.9.44	
	Mourmelon-le-Grand (F)	16.10.44	
	Toul (F)	20.11.44	
	Mannheim/Sandhofen (G)	7.4.44	
	Reims (F)	23.6.45	—10.7.45
Aircraft:	P-47		
Squadron markings:	365th FS: White cowling, fin and rudder		
	366th FS: Yellow cowling, fin and rudder		
	367th FS: Red cowling, fin and rudder		

P-47 'Chunky' of the 358th FG receives attention [IWM neg. EA29281]

362nd FIGHTER GROUP

Although the 362nd FG had arrived in England at the end of November 1943, its first mission, escorting B-24s of the 8th Air Force bombing V.1 sites in the Pas de Calais, was not until 8 February 1944. The Group's main task until it moved to an ALG in Kent in April 1944 continued to be the escort role, but during April and May the shorter flying distance enabled it to attack communications targets in France and Belgium. On D-Day the Group's P-47s escorted C-47s of IX TCC carrying paratroops to Normandy and afterwards was involved principally in close-support work, strafing targets chosen by the ground forces to assist their advance.

In July 1944 the 362nd left England and moved to France to support the Allied advance toward Germany. A DUC was awarded for the Group's low-level missions to Brest on 25 August, when a successful attack on shipping, naval installations and other targets was made. The Group then took part in the Battle of the Bulge and received another DUC, this time for activity over the river Rhine on 16 March, when a wide variety of targets was strafed and wiped out.

The 362nd FG's final operation took place on 1 May 1945, and the Group returned home in August and September.

P-47s of the 362nd FG's 378th FS at an airstrip in France

[via author]

Squadrons and codes:	377th FS [E4]	
	378th FS [G8]	
	379th FS [B8]	
Bases:	Wormingford	30.11.43
	Headcorn	15.4.44
	Lignerolles (F)	7.7.44
	Rennes (F)	12.8.44
	Prosnes (F)	22.9.44
	Rouvres (F)	11.44
	Frankfurt (G)	4.45
	Furth (G)	30.4.45
	Illesheim (G)	4.5.45
	Straubing (G)	15.5.45-
		—8.45
Aircraft:	P-47	
Squadron markings:	377th FS: Red nose band and red upper fin and rudder	
	378th FS: Green nose band and red upper fin and rudder	
	379th FS: Yellow nose band and red upper fin and rudder	

363rd FIGHTER GROUP

Christmas 1943 saw the arrival in England of the 363rd FG, fresh from training in California. P-51 aircraft were received in January 1944 and the Group's first operation was mounted on 23 February. For the next four months the Group escorted bombers and fighter-bombers to their targets in France, Germany, Belgium and Holland and also strafed strategic targets.

On D-Day, 6 June 1944, the 363rd escorted IX TCC C-47s towing CG-4 gliders over Normandy, and attacked front-line positions. At the end of June a move was made to France to enable the Group to take a closer part in the Allied advance. This it did, but on 4 September was redesignated the 363rd Tactical Reconnaissance Group in order to take on a new role.

Squadrons and codes:	380th FS [A9]		
	381st FS [B3]		
	382nd FS [C3]		
Bases:	Keevil	23.12.43	
	Rivenhall	1.44	
	Staplehurst	4.44	
	Maupertus (F)	1.7.44	
	Azeville (F)	8.44	→
Commanding Officers:	Col. John R. Ulricson		
	Col. James B. Tipton	7.5.44	
	Col. James M. Smelley	1.9.44	→
Aircraft:	P-51		
Squadron markings:	380th FS: Blue spinner and nose tip; black horizontal band across fin and rudder		
	381st FS: Yellow spinner and nose tip; black horizontal band across fin and rudder		
	382nd FS: Red spinner and nose tip; black horizontal band across fin and rudder		

P-51B 2106485 [A9:V], 'Maggie's Drawers', of the 380th FS, 363rd FG, heads out on a mission [H. Holmes]

Coded C3:F, P-51B 36830 of the 363rd FG's 382nd FS [D. Benfield]

P-51D 413811 'Big Mac Junior' of the 363rd FG at Staplehurst ALG, surrounded by contented-looking pilots and ground crews   [via H. Holmes]

363rd TACTICAL RECONNAISSANCE GROUP

On 4 September 1944 the 363rd FG was redesignated the 363rd TRG and took on a new role, flying F-5 and F-6 aircraft in support of the newly-formed US Ninth Army. The three squadrons were renumbered as the 160th, 161st and 162nd TRS, and to them was added the 33rd PRS, previously part of the 67th TRG. The tasks now performed included directing fighter-bombers to their targets, adjusting artillery fire, photographing future targets and damage asessment sorties. In this role the Group assisted the Ninth Army's drive across the Rhine and into Germany in the final month of the War, which also saw some squadron movements.

In June 1945, the war over, the word 'Tactical' was dropped from the Group's title, but this was purely academic as the squadrons soon began to be dispersed among other Groups or to return to the USA.

Squadrons and codes:	33rd PRS [2W]	(see note A)		
	160th TRS [A9]	(see note B)		
	161st TRS [B3]	(see note C)		
	162nd TRS [C3]	(see note D)		
Bases (HQ):	Le Mans (F)		9.44	
	Sandweiler (L)		1.10.44	
	Le Culot (B)		29.10.44	
	Venlo (H)		3.45	
	Gutersloh (G)		15. 4.45	
	Braunschweig (G)		22. 4.45	
	Wiesbaden (G)		5.45	
	Eschwege (G)		8.45	
	Darmstadt (G)		9.45	— 2.12.45
Bases (Squadrons):				
33rd PRS:	Gosselies (B)		21. 9.44	
	Le Culot (B)		5.11.44	
	Venlo (H)		10. 3.45	
	Gutersloh (G)		16. 4.45	
	Braunshweig (G)		25. 4.45	
160th TRS:	Montreuil (F)		9. 9.44	
	Sandweiler (L)		11.10.44	
	Le Culot (B)		29.10.44	
	Venlo (H)		11. 3.45	
	Gutersloh (G)		16. 4.45	
	Braunschweig (G)		26.4.45	
	Wiesbaden (G)		20. 5.45	
	Eschwege (G)		12. 7.45	
	Darmstadt (G)		22. 9.45	— 15.11.45

161st TRS:	Montreuil (F)	11. 9.44	
	Sandweiler (L)	2.10.44	
	Le Culot (B)	31.10.44	
	Venlo (H)	11. 3.45	
	Gutersloh (G)	16. 4.45	
	Braunschweig (G)	26. 4.45	
	Wiesbaden (G)	19. 5.45	— 3. 7.45
162nd TRS:	Montreuil (F)	13. 9.44	— 24. 9.44
Commanding Officers:	Col. James M. Smelley	4.9.44	
	Lt. Col. Seth A. Mize	5.45	— N/K

Aircraft:

33rd PRS:	F-5; P-38
160th TRS:	F-6; P-51
161st TRS:	F-6; P-51
162nd TRS:	F-6; P-51

Notes on 363rd TRG squadrons:

(A) Transferred from 67th TRG 30.10.44; re-assigned to 67th TRG for the period 17.5.45 to 5.7.45 and returned to 67th TRG 20.8.45

(B) Air echelon attached to 10th PG 24.12.44 to 6.2.45. Transferred to 10th PG 15.11.45

(C) Air echelon attached to 10th PG 23.12.44 to 3.1.45. Transferred to 67th TRG 3.7.45

(D) Transferred to 10th RG 29.9.44

Squadron markings: 160th TRS: Light blue spinnner and nose band
161st TRS: Yellow spinner and nose band
162nd TRS: Red spinner and nose band

365th FIGHTER GROUP

The 365th FG moved to England in December 1943 and began combat operations with P-47s in February 1944. From that time the Group was involved in escort and fighter-bomber missions up to D-Day +1, when it mounted an all-out strike on enemy defences behind Omaha Beach and beyond. Late in June, the 365th moved to France to concentrate on assisting Allied ground forces in their drive across France.

In September 1944 the 365th FG flew patrols in connection with airborne operations over Holland and was awarded a citation by the Belgian Government for its work in the liberation of Belgium. Soon afterwards came a DUC for shooting down a large number of enemy aircraft in the Bonn/Dusseldorf area on 21 October. During the Battle of the Bulge a second Belgian citation was received by the 365th, for its concentrated attacks on railway yards, factories and gun batteries. While the crossing of the river Rhine was made, the Group provided aerial cover and then supported the advance into Germany. A second DUC was awarded to the 365th for its efforts on 20 April 1945, when it attacked targets in southern Germany, but this was almost the last mission of the war for the Group.

The 365th FG participated in the disarmament programme in Germany for a few weeks before returning home in September 1945.

Squadrons and codes:	386th FS [D5]		
	387th FS [B4]		
	388th FS [C4]		
Bases:	Gosfield	22.12.43	
	Beaulieu	5. 3.44	
	Azeville (F)	28. 6.44	
	Lignerolles (F)	8.44	
	Bretigny (F)	3. 9.44	
	Juvincourt (F)	14. 9.44	
	Chievres (B)	4.10.44	
	Metz (F)	29.12.44	
	Florennes/Juzaines (B)	30. 1.45	
	Aachen (G)	16. 3.45	
	Fritzlar (G)	13. 4.45	
	Suippes (F)	29. 7.45	
	Antwerp (B)	22.8.45	—11.9.45
Commanding Officers:	Col. Lance Call		
	Col. Ray J. Stecker	26. 6.44	
	Lt. Col. Robert C. Richardson III	26. 4.45	—N/K
Aircraft:	P-47		
Squadron markings:	386th FS: Red noseband		
	387th FS: Yellow noseband		
	388th FS: White noseband		

366th FIGHTER GROUP

One of the many FGs which arrived in England in December 1943 and January 1944, the 366th spent some weeks becoming used to European conditions before entering combat on 14 March 1944 with a fighter sweep along the coast of France. The Group then concentrated on 'softening-up' operations, preparing the way for the invasion of Europe on 6 June 1944, on which day it flew dawn fighter-bomber sweeps over Normandy and attacked road convoys and gun batteries near the beachhead.

Soon after D-Day the 366th FG moved to France to concentrate on divebombing missions against lines of communication and fortiffied areas. On such a mission on 11 July, aircraft of the Group spotted an unreported enemy tank column, and in driving rain and heavy flak inflicted severe damage on it. For this the Group was awarded a DUC.

Other operations in which the 366th took part included the support of Alied armour during the St. Lo breakthrough in July 1944; an attack on flak positions near Eindhoven during the airborne operations in September; the Battle of the Bulge in December 1944 and January 1945; and the escort of bombers during the Rhine crossing in March. The Group's final mission was an attack on Kiel and Flensburg harbours five days before the war in Europe ended.

After the war, the 366th FG remained in Germany, passing out of 9th Air Force control on 2 December 1945.

Squadrons and codes:	389th FS [A6]		
	390th FS [B2]		
	391st FS [A8]		
Bases:	Membury	10.1.44	
	Thruxton	1.3.44	
	St. Pierre du Mont (F)	17.6.44	
	Dreux (F)	24.8.44	
	Laon/Couvron (F)	8.9.44	
	Asch (B)	20.11.44	
	Munster/Handorf (G)	14.4.44	
	Bayreuth/Bindlach (G)	25.6.44	
	Fritzlar (G)	14.9.45	→
Commanding Officers:	Col. Dyke F. Meyer		
	Lt. Col. James P. Tipton	19.4.44	
	Lt. Col. Donald K. Bennett	30.4.44	
	Col. Harold N. Holt	22.5.44	
	Lt. Col. Ansel J. Wheeler	28.4.45	→
Aircraft:	P-47		
Group marking:	Horizontal band across fin and rudder		

367th FIGHTER GROUP

Although the 367th FG had trained on P-39s in the United States, the Group was issued with P-38s soon after arrival in England in April 1944 and continued to use them for a year. The 367th entered the fray on 9 May 1944 in a strike role, concentrating on targets in western France, but also escorted heavy bombers to the same area. From D-Day on, the Group provided cover for the Allied forces crossing the Channel and then strafed a variety of targets behind the invasion beaches.

In July 1944 the 367th moved to France and continued to operate in support of ground forces, largely to prevent enemy supplies from reaching the front line. A mission on 25 August, when the Group's aircraft attacked enemy airfields through heavy flak and strafed a train and a road convoy on the way home, was rewarded with a DUC. During the autumn of 1944 the Group took part in the Allied drive across the Siegfried line, and on Boxing Day escorted C-47s dropping supplies to Allied troops under siege at Bastogne.

The 367th FG relinquished its P-38s in February 1945 in favour of P-47s, with which it secured another DUC for an attack on the heavily- defended HQ of the German C-in-C West at Ziegenburg. Toward the end of hostilities the 367th supported the assault across the Rhine and the drive into Germany, flying its last mission on VE-Day, 8 May 1945. A return to the USA was made during July and August 1945 for de-activation later that year.

Squadrons and codes:	392nd FS [H5]		
	393rd FS [8L]		
	394th FS [4N]		
Bases:	Stoney Cross	5.4.44	
	Ibsley	6.7.44	
	Beuzeville (F)**	22.7.44	
	Criqueville (F)	14.8.44	
	Peray (F)	5.9.44	
	Clastres (F)	8.9.44	
	Juvincourt (F)	28.10.44	
	St. Dizier (F)	1.2.45	
	Conflans (F)	14.3.45	
	Frankfurt/Eschborn (G)	10.4.45	—7.45

** HQ only; squadrons at Carentan, Cretteville and St. Mere-Eglise.

Commanding Officers:	Col. Charles M. Young		
	Col. Edwin S. Chickering	9.11.44	—N/K
Aircraft:	P-38 (4.44 — 2.45)		
	P-47 (2.45 — 7.45)		

Squadron markings:

392nd FS	P-38s:	Black triangle on tailplane; red nose tip and spinner
	P-47s:	Red cowling and red/yellow/blue upper fin and rudder
393rd FS	P-38s:	Black circle on tailplane; blue nose tip and spinner
	P-47s:	Blue cowling and red/yellow/blue upper fin and rudder
394th FS	P-38s:	Black square on tailplane; yellow nose tip and spinner
	P-47s:	Yellow cowling and red/yellow/blue upper fin and rudder

368th FIGHTER GROUP

The 368th FG arrived in England in January 1944 and commenced operations on 14 March with a fighter sweep over the French coast. Between then and D-Day the Group made strafing attacks on lines of communication, airfields, flak positions and V-weapon sites in preparation for the invasion. Support was given to the Allied troops during the landings, particularly on D+1, when V Corps was isolated on the beach. Very soon, the Group moved to France to be nearer the action.

Once the invasion forces were established, the 368th took part in the capture of Cherbourg and the breakthrough at St. Lo, and then supported the troops in their drive across France. The Group was awarded a DUC for its support operations around Mons on 3 September, when its P-47s destroyed large numbers of vehicles and wiped out pockets of enemy resistance that were impeding Allied progress. Support of the ground forces continued right across France and Belgium, finally ending when the Rhine had been crossed. After VE-Day, the 368th FG remained in Germany up to and beyond the de-activation of the 9th Air Force in December 1945.

Squadrons and codes:	395th FS [A7]		
	396th FS [C2]		
	397th FS [D3]		
Bases:	Greenham Common	13.1.44	
	Chilbolton	15.3.44	
	Cardonville (F)	20.6.44	
	Chartres (F)	23.8.44	
	Laon/Athies (F)	11.9.44	
	Chievres (B)	2.10.44	
	Juvincourt (F)	27.12.44	
	Metz (F)	5.1.45	
	Frankfurt-am-Main (G)	15.4.45	
	Buchschwabach (G)	13.5.45	
	Straubing (G)	13.8.45	→
Commanding Officers:	Col. Gilbert L. Meyers		
	Col. Frank S. Perego	1.11.44	
	Maj. Dennis Crisp	18.10.45	
	Lt. Col. John L. Locke	2.11.45	→
Aircraft:	P-47		

Squadron markings:
395th FS: Red noseband and upper fin and rudder above black horizontal band
396th FS: Yellow noseband and upper fin and rudder above black horizontal band
397th FS: Blue noseband and upper fin and rudder above black horizontal band

370th FIGHTER GROUP

Arriving in England in February 1944, the 370th FG was soon issued with P-38s, although it had trained on P-47s in the USA. The Group entered combat on 1 May 1944, and began a sustained series of dive-bombing attacks on radar stations and flak towers as well as escorting bombers raiding bridges and railway yards in the run-up to the invasion of France.

On D-Day the 370th gave cover to the cross-Channel movement of shipping and aircraft, and for the rest of June flew armed reconnaissance sorties over the Cotentin peninsula. In July the Group moved to France and concentrated on hitting gun batteries, supply dumps, tank and troop movements, particularly near St. Lo in July and Falaise in August. Some of the Group's aircraft and pilots were detached to England in September 1944 to provide cover for the airborne assault on Holland, but they returned in time to join in the lst Army's capture of Aachen early in October. A DUC was awarded to the 370th for a mission in support of the ground forces on 2 December 1944, when napalm bombs were dropped on a heavily-defended village, inflicting severe casualties on enemy troops.

Armed reconnaissance sorties were again flown by the 370th FG during the Battle of the Bulge around Christmas 1944, but in February and March 1945 the Group forsook its faithful P-38s to convert onto P-51s. With these the Group attacked bridges and docks around Wesel and patrolled the area while paratroops were dropped on the east bank of the Rhine on 24 March. During April 1945 support was given to the 2nd Armoured Division in the Ruhr valley, and the 370th FG's final mission, a sweep over Dessau and Wittenberg, was made on 4 May 1945.

The 370th FG returned to the USA over a period of time between September and November 1945 to be inactivated.

A P-38 coded 7F:Q of the 370th FG

[Merle Olmsted]

Squadrons and codes:	401st FS [9D]		
	402nd FS [E6]		
	485th FS [7F]		
Bases:	Aldermaston	12.2.44	
	Andover	29.2.44	
	Cardonville (F)	31.7.44	
	La Vielle (F)	15.8.44	
	Lonray (F)	6.9.44	
	Roye/Amy (F)	11.9.44	
	Florennes/Juzaines (B)	26.9.44	
	Zwartberg (B)	27.1.45	
	Gutersloh (G)	20.4.45	
	Mannheim/Sandhofen (G)	27.6.45	
	Fritzlar (G)	6.8.45	—9.45
Commanding Officers:	Col. Howard F. Nichols		
	Lt. Col. Seth J. McKee	6.11.44	
	Lt. Col. Morgan A. Giffin	22.2.45	
	Col. Seth J. McKee	10.5.45	—9.45
Aircraft:	P-38 (2.44—2.45)		
	P-51 (2.45—9.45)		

Squadron markings:

401st FS	P-38s:	White square on tailplane; yellow and blue spinner
	P-51s:	Yellow spinner and nose tip and horizontal band across fin and rudder
402nd FS	P-38s:	White circle on tailplane; blue and white spinner
	P-51s:	Dark blue spinner and nose tip and diagonal band across fin and rudder
485th FS	P-38s:	White triangle on fin and rudder; red and blue spinner
	P-51s:	Red spinner and nose tip and vertical band on fin

Another of the many Fighter Groups which arrived in England early in 1944 to join the 9th Air Force, the 371st began operations on 12 April 1944 with a fighter sweep over France. For the next few weeks the Group flew strafing, escort and sweeping sorties until D-Day, when its P-47s joined in the concerted attacks on trains, vehicles, gun emplacements and other targets and patrolled the beachheads. Due to heavy wear on the temporary runways at Bisterne, however, the three squadrons used lbsley airfield between 28 April and 14 May.

After D-Day, the 371st continued its operations, now from French airstrips in supporting the Allied advance across France and, in the autumn of 1944 and the winter it operated over north-east France and south-western Germany, attacking a wide variety of strategic targets. A DUC was received for the Group's activities between 15 and 21 March 1945, a six-day operation bent on destroying as much of the German transportation system as possible, together with factories and gun positions.

The war in Europe over, the 371st FG returned home to the USA in October and November 1945.

Bubble-cockpit P-47D 227376 [9Q:R] of the 371st FG's 404th FS at rest on a PSP hardstand in France [IWM neg. EA48944]

Squadrons and codes:	404th FS [9Q]		
	405th FS [8N]		
	406th FS [4W]		
Bases:	Bisterne	7.3.44	
	Beuzeville (F)	17.6.44	
	Perthes (F)	18.9.44	
	Dole/Tavaux (F)	1.10.44	
	Tantonville (F)	20.12.44	
	Metz (F)	15.2.45	
	Frankfurt/Eschborn (G)	7.4.45	
	Furth (G)	5.5.45	
	Horsching (A)	16.8.45	
	Stuttgart (G)	13.9.45	—10.45
Commanding Officers:	Col. Bingham T. Kleine		
	Lt. Col. William P. McBride	9.45	—N/K
Aircraft:	P-47		
Squadron markings:			
	404th FS: Red noseband, later cowling, light blue fin and rudder		
	405th FS: Blue noseband, later cowling		
	406th FS: Yellow noseband, later cowling		

373rd FIGHTER GROUP

One of the later arrivals in England, the 373rd FG was based at Woodchurch, an ALG in Kent, from April 1944. The Group's P-47s flew their first operation, a fighter sweep over Normandy, on 8 May and followed this with a series of escort duties for B-26s attacking airfields, railway yards and bridges in the area of the forthcoming invasion of France. On D-Day the Group flew patrols over the beachhead and struck against a variety of strategic targets until the end of June.

In July 1944 the 373rd FG left England for France to enable it to press home its attacks deeper into enemy territory, con-centrating on preventing reinforcements reaching the front line. Subsequently, the 373rd followed the Allied movement over France and into Germany, taking part in the Battle of the Bulge in December 1944 and January 1945 and the Rhine crossing in March 1945. On 20 March the Group's P-47s fiercely attacked enemy airfields east of the Rhine, notwithstanding very heavy AA fire, greatly helping the Allied armies, and for this was awarded a DUC.

Tactical air strikes were continued until 4 May, and the 373rd returned to the USA in July 1945.

Squadrons and codes:	410th FS [R3]	Group marking:	Black noseband and horizontal
	411th FS [U9]	band across fin and rudder	
	412th FS [V5]		
Bases:	Woodchurch	4.4.44	
	Tour-en-Bessin (F)	30.7.44	
	St. James (F)	20.8.44	
	Reims (F)	9.44	
	Le Culot (B)	24.10.44	
	Venlo (H)	14.3.45	
	Lippstadt (G)	20.4.45	
	Illesheim (G)	20.5.45;	—7.45
Commanding Officers:	Col. William H. Schwartz Jr.		
	Col. James C. McGehee	17.11.44	
	Lt. Col. James F. McCarthy	5.45	—N/K
Aircraft:	P-47		

At Woodchurch ALG, a truck-load of drop-tanks is driven past a dispersal point on which stands P-47D 227627 of the 373rd FG   [via Alan Wright]

A 412th FS (373rd FG) P-47D, V5:N, just made it home to make a wheels-up land-ing, the pilot luckily not being hurt
[Bill Mather via Alan Wright]

Transferred from the 8th Air Force in October 1943, the 386th BG was based at Great Dunmow and had flown its first mission in July 1943. Originally the Group had concentrated its efforts on attacking enemy airfields, with railway yards and defensive positions as a sideline. During the winter of 1944/45, however, an intensive campaign against V.1 sites in the Pas de Calais was carried on, and in the last week of February 1944 airfields in Holland and Belgium felt the effects of the 386th BG's B-26s.

In the spring of 1944 the 386th BG contributed to the 'softening-up' of northern France by bombing many of the Seine bridges, railway depots and airfields, while on D-Day itself the Group concentrated on eliminating coastal gun batteries. Thenceforth relentless attacks on strategic targets behind enemy lines were maintained, and a contribution to the assault on the enemy at St. Lo was made. In August the Group destroyed targets in the Falaise area to help clear the German forces, and hit strong points in the port of Brest during Sep-

tember. During that month one of the 386th BG's squadrons, the 553rd, became the first squadron in the ETO to convert onto the new Douglas A-26 aircraft.

A move to France came in October 1944, enabling the Group to penetrate further into enemy territory. During the Battle of the Bulge, bridges were the 386th's main targets, so that enemy supply lines could be cut.

Soon after the Ardennes campaign, the 386th relinquished the remainder of its B-26s in order to convert onto A-26s, with which it continued to strike hard against strategic targets in Germany. During one sortie on 19 February 1945, Maj. Myron L. Durkee was credited with the 'probable' destruction of a Me.262 jet fighter, having demonstrated the nimble handling capability of the A-26.

The Group's title was altered slightly to 'Light' in June 1945, but soon after this the 386th began to return to the USA for deactivation.

A 386th BG B-26 climbs away over the heads of British workmen. Note censorship of part of the fuselage. [IWM neg. KY10865]

Four A-26s of the 552nd BS, 386th BG, formating on an RAF Lancaster early in 1945. Tail numbers and codes were: 139317 [RG:X], 139343 [RG:Y], 322318 [RG:L] and 322483 [RG:P] [via J. J. Halley]

A-26B 139186 [AN:W] of the 386th BG's 553rd BS, which began to convert onto the type in September 1944, just before leaving England   [via D. Smith]

Squadrons and codes:	552nd BS [RG]	**Group marking:** yellow horizontal stripe across fin and rudder
	553rd BS [AN]	
	554th BS [RU]	
	555th BS [YA]	
Bases:	Great Dunmow	24.9.43
	Beaumont-sur-Oise (F)	2.10.44
	St. Trond (B)	9.4.45 —27.7.45
Commanding Officers:	Col. Lester J. Maitland	
	Col. Richard C. Sanders	18.11.43
	Col. Joe W. Kelly	22.1.44
Aircraft:	B-26; A-26 (553rd BS from 9.44, other sqdns. from 1.45)	

387th BOMBARDMENT GROUP (MEDIUM)

B-26G 334186 [FW:P] 'Los Lobos Grandes III' of the 556th BS, 387th BG [Jack Molloy via D. W. Crouchman]

Another of the original 9th Air Force Bomb Groups, the 387th had arrived in England in June 1943 and was assigned to the 8th Air Force until October. Combat missions, mainly against enemy airfields, had begun in August 1943, but after transferring to the 9th Air Force the Group made many strikes against V.1 sites in northern France during the winter of 1943/44. The intensive assault against the Luftwaffe and the German aircraft industry in February 1944 saw the 387th taking part, after which the Group switched its efforts to the 'softening-up' campaign which was mounted in April and May in preparation for the forthcoming invasion of France.

On D-Day the 387th BG attacked coastal gun emplacements and subsequently supported the ground troops in breaking out from the beach-heads. The Group moved to France in July 1944 and continued to aid the ground forces in their drive across France and into Germany, taking part in the Ardennes campaign, for which a DUC for meritorious effort was received. Support continued to be given to the Allied forces until the 387th's final mission was flown at the end of April 1945.

After VE-Day, the 387th BG remained in France until returning home in November 1945 to be de-activated.

B-26Bs 295934 [TQ:P] 'Mrs Ironhead' and 295869 [TQ:F] 'The Front Burner II', of the 559th BS, 387th BG

[R. Hambly via D. W. Crouchman]

Squadrons and codes:	556th BS [FW]		Group marking: yellow/black horizontal stripe across fin and rudder	
	557th BS [KS]			
	558th BS [KX]			
	559th BS [TQ]			
Bases:	Chipping Ongar	1.7.43		
	Stoney Cross	21.7.44		
	Maupertus (F)	1.9.44		
	Chateaudun (F)	18.9.44		
	Clastres (F)	4.11.44		
	Maastricht/Beek (H)	4.5.45		
	Rosieres-en-Santerres (F)	30.5.45	−11.45	
Commanding Officers:	Col. Carl L. Storrie			
	Col. Jack E. Caldwell	8.11.43		
	Col. Thomas M. Seymour	13.4.44		
	Col. Grover C. Brown	18.7.44		
	Lt. Col. Richard R. Stewart	20.5.45		
	Col. Phillip A. Sykes	6.45	−N/K	
Aircraft:	B-26			

391st BOMBARDMENT GROUP (MEDIUM)

The 391st BG converted onto the A-26 in April 1945; 322616, an A-26C, is an example [R. Mynn]

After arrival in England in January 1944, the 391st BG entered combat within two weeks and concentrated on strategic targets in northern France, Belgium and Holland, including V-weapon sites. On D-Day, the Group's B-26s strafed coastal gun batteries, shooting down in the process a Fw190 over Point du Hoc, and followed this by a continued concentrated campaign of destroying fuel dumps and troop concentrations, with attacks also on lines of communication.

In September 1944 the 391st left England for a base on the Continent, from where the Group's operations could be extended into the German heartland. Over the period of Christmas 1944 the Battle of the Bulge took place in the Ardennes, and the 391st played its part in attacking heavily fortified enemy positions, for which a DUC was awarded. In the new year, the Group concentrated in destroying the German transportation system, using A-26 aircraft during the final few weeks of hostilities. The Group's final operation was flown on 3 May 1945, and it was redesignated 391st BG (Light) in July before returning to the USA in September and October 1945 for de-activation.

Squadrons and codes:	572nd BS [P2]	**Group marking:** yellow triangle on fin
	573rd BS [T6]	and rudder
	574th BS [4L]	
	575th BS [08]	
Bases:	Matching	26.1.44
	Roye/Amy (F)	9.44
	Asch (B)	20.4.45
	Vitry-en-Artois (F)	1.6.45
	Laon (F)	27.7.45	—9.45
Commanding Officers:	Col. Gerald E. Williams	26.1.44	—9.45
Aircraft:	B-26 (1.44 - 4.45); A-26 (4.45 - 7.45)	

B-26B 295808 'Idiot's Delight' certainly needed a new paint job when seen in this pre-D-Day shot   [R. Mynn]

A B-26C at rest: 2107673 coded P2:A, seen at Matching just before D-Day, was shot down on 8 August 1944 [R. Mynn]

B-26C 2107810 [T6:W] on finals at Matching [R. Mynn]

Typical of different colour schemes within a Group are the natural metal finish of 2107620 [08:B] and the olive drab of P2:U, both of the 391st BG

[R. Mynn]

394th BOMBARDMENT GROUP (MEDIUM)

B-26B 296085 [K5:M] 'El Salvo' of 394th
BG under major repair at Boreham
[via Bryan Jones]

The 394th BG moved to England in March 1944 after training on B-26s in the United States, and began a series of operations against V-weapon sites, railway yards, airfields, bridges and defences almost at once. On D-Day, the Group's aircraft attacked gun batteries at Cherbourg and elsewhere and then concentrated on fuel dumps and lines of communication in Normandy. Four aircraft and 23 men were lost on D-Day; all crashed in England after striking gun emplacements at St. Martin de Varreville, the 58th mission for the Group. Most unfortunate of all was the mid-air collision over Gillingham, Kent, between two aircraft of the Group's 587th BS, while another aircraft of the same squadron came down in Ashburnham Park, Sussex and one of the 584th BS's aircraft crashed at nearby Battle.

The Group, known by now as the 'Bridge Busters', was awarded a DUC by Lt. Gen. Lewis H. Brereton, Commanding General of the 9th Air Force, on 14 January 1944 after a very successful mission against a railway bridge near Cloyes in which 36 394th BG B-26s took part. This bridge formed one of the most important links between the Seine and Loire rivers, and was demolished in a fine piece of precision bombing. One B-26 was lost to heavy AA.fire.

Further successful missions for which commendation was received were the elimination of heavy gun positions at Fort d'Octeville, near Cherbourg, on 24 June, allowing ground troops to resume their advance, and partrcipation in the St. Lo breakthrough on 25 July.

This was the final mission carried out from the Group's base at Boreham. On 17 July an advance party had left for Holmsley South in Hampshire, and a week later the main party made the journey to the new base. The remainder of the Group arrived at Holmsley South on 27 July, and the 394th was now better able to cope with targets ahead of the ground forces advancing over Normandy.

Missions flown from Holmsley South included the destruction of an ammunition dump and railway bridges between 7 and 9 August, for which one of the formation leaders received a Medal of Honour. A further move was made toward the end of August 1944, when the 394th found itself in France. From its new base the Group attacked the port of Brest and targets in Germany, as well as taking part in the Battle of the Bulge in December 1944 and January 1945. From that time until the end of the war in Europe the Group continued its relentless campaign, principally against transportation facilities, and also dropped propaganda leaflets.

After the war, the 394th BG remained in Europe, and was still based in Germany when the 9th Air Force was inactivated in December 1945.

Squadrons and codes:	584th BS [K5]	**Group marking:** white diagonal stripe	
	585th BS [4T]	across fin and rudder	
	586th BS [H9]		
	587th BS [5W]		
Bases:	Boreham	11.3.44	
	Holmsley South	24.7.44	
	Tour-en-Bessin (F)	20.8.44	
	Orleans/Bricy (F)	18.9.44	
	Cambrai/Niergnies (F)	8.10.44	
	Venlo (H)	2.5.45	
	Kitzingen (G)	9.45	→
Commanding Officers:	Col. Thomas B. Hall		
	Col. Gove C. Celio Jr.	24.1.45	→
Aircraft:	B-26		

A late model B-26G, 467835, of the 586th BS, 394th BG, over its target

[via Bryan Jones]

397th BOMBARDMENT GROUP (MEDIUM)

One of the last Bomb Groups to come to England, the 397th did not arrive until April 1944, but quickly settled down to a routine of attacks on railway depots, airfields and bridges in the area of the impending invasion and on V.1 sites in the Pas de Calais. The Group's B-26s strafed fortified positions on D-Day, and then supported the Allied armies in their advance across France.

In August 1944 the 397th moved to France to be nearer the action, and bombed targets at St. Malo, Brest and Rouen. Missions over Germany were begun in September. During the Battle of the Bulge the Group was awarded a DUC for destroying a vital bridge in the face of sustained flak and fighter defences. Subsequently, the 397th continued to support the Allied armies until the end of hostilities, and remained in France until December 1945.

Squadrons and codes:	596th BS [X2]	**Group marking:** yellow horizontal
	597th BS [9F]	stripe edged black across fin and rudder
	598th BS [U2]	
	599th BS [6B]	
Bases:	Gosfield	5.4.44
	Rivenhall	15.4.44
	Hurn	4.8.44
	Gorges (F)	30.8.44
	Dreux (F)	15.9.44
	Peronne (F)	7.10.44
	Venlo (H)	25.4.45
	Peronne (F)	30.5.45 —12.45
Commanding Officers:	Col. Richard T. Coiner Jr.	
	Lt. Col. Jimmie W. Britt	23.7.45 N/K
Aircraft:	B-26 (4.44); A-26	

A 'sharkmouth' decoration on a 397th BG B-26

B-26B 296191 [9F:N] of the 397th BG's
597th BS   [B. Stait]

404th FIGHTER GROUP

Known as the 404th Fighter-Bomber Group on arrival in England in March and April 1944, the Group's title was modified in May 1944. It became operational on the first day of that month, participating in the preparations for the invasion of Europe by strafing strategic targets in France. On 9 May the Group mounted its first, fairly successful, mission against V.1 sites.

The 404th provided top cover over the beachheads on D-Day, and a further major effort was made on 10 June by 48 of the Group's aircraft which attacked railways, bridges and artillery positions in Normandy. Subsequently the 404th continued to operate close-support missions for the Allied armies, moving to France in July 1944 to make the task easier. Escort sorties were

also flown, covering the operation of heavy and medium bombers raiding factories, airfields, railway depots and other targets. Several citations were awarded to the 404th FG during this period. For aiding the First Army at St. Lo at the end of July despite heavy losses from flak, a French Croix de Guerre with Palm Leaves was awarded, and a DUC for three armed reconnaissance missions on 10 September was received. The Belgian Government also cited the 404th, for help in freeing the Belgian people.

After the end of hostilities, the 404th FG took part in the dismantling of the German aircraft industry and Luftwaffe before returning home in August 1945.

'My Mozelle' is a P-47 coded 7J:E of the
404th FG's 508th FS   [Merle Olmsted]

Squadrons and codes:	506th FS [4K]	**Group marking:** White noseband and	
	507th FS [Y8]	horizontal band across fin and rudder	
	508th FS [7J]		
Bases:	Winkton	5.4.44	
	Chapelle (F)	6.7.44	
	Bretigny (F)	29.8.44	
	Juvincourt (F)	13.9.44	
	St. Trond (B)	1.10.44	
	Kelz (G)	30.3.45	
	Fritzlar (G)	12.4.45	
	Stuttgart (G)	23.6.45	—8.45
Commanding Officers:	Col. Carroll W. McColpin		
	Lt. Col. Leo C. Moon	25.11.44	
	Lt. Col. John R. Murphy	23.4.45	—N/K
Aircraft:	P-47		

Seen parked in the snow is P-47D 227221
[4K:L] of the 404th FG's 506th FS
[Merle Olmsted]

405th FIGHTER GROUP

Another minor mishap. P-47D coded
K4:D, 'Nancy' of the 405th FG's 511th
FS, being studies by a number of GIs.
[IWM neg. EA47887]

Following its arrival in England early in March 1944, the 405th FBG, equipped with P-47s, entered combat on 11 April before being redesignated as the 405th FG in May. Before D-Day the Group spent its time fruitfully in bombing airfields, railway yards and bridges, but on the big day patrols over the Brest area were flown, followed by armed reconnaissance missions supporting the recently-landed ground forces.

At the end of June the 405th moved to France to continue support missions for the advancing Allied armies. It took part in the St. Lo offensive in July and was awarded a DUC for a dangerous mission on 24 September in support of the Third Army. Two of the three squadrons, flying in very bad weather, were directed to a tank battle, but only one squadron located and strafed the tanks. The other squadron attacked a military convoy instead. Later that day, the Group's third squadron strafed storage points in the same area.

For its part in the liberation of Belgium, the 405th was cited by the Belgian Government. The last operation for the 405th was flown on VE-Day, 8 May 1945, and the Group began to return to the USA in July.

Squadrons and codes:	509th FS [G9]		
	510th FS [2Z]		
	511th FS [K4]		
Bases:	Christchurch	7.3.44	
	Picauville (F)	30.6.44	
	St. Dizier (F)	13.9.44	
	Ophoven (B)	9.2.45	
	Kitzingen (G)	23.4.45	
	Straubing (G)	8.5.45	—7.45
Commanding Officers:	Col. James Ferguson		
	Col. Robert L. Delashaw	26.4.44	
	Lt. Col. J. Garrett Jackson	22.10.44	—N/K
Aircraft:	P-47		
Squadron markings:	507th FS: Red noseband and horizontal band across fin and rudder		
	510th FS: Blue noseband and horizontal band across fin and rudder		
	511th FS: Yellow noseband and horizontal band across fin and rudder		

406th FIGHTER GROUP

The 406th FBG arrived in England in April 1944 and settled down at Ashford, one of the ALGs in Kent. Roughly coincident with the Group's entry into battle was its redesignation as the 406th Fighter Group in May 1944.

After providing aerial cover during the D-Day landings, the 406th flew strafing and armed reconnaissance missions over Normandy and took part in the breakthrough at St. Lo on 25 July. Early in August the Group left its temporary home and moved to an even more temporary one in France to continue its tactical support role. Brest and St. Malo were particular targets that month, and the Group's rocket-equipped P-47s were prominent on 7 September in destroying a large convoy of enemy vehicles attempting to escape, an action for which a DUC was received. One of the 406th FG's squadrons, the 513th, claimed to have destroyed the first V.1 flying bomb shot down by the USAAF.

Operating closely with the ground forces, the 406th took part in the drive towards the Saar area, but switched operations to the Ardennes during the Battle of the Bulge in December 1944. Flying within a small area during that campaign, the Group was awarded a second DUC for its efforts. Towards the end of hostilities, the 406th aided ground troops in the crossing of the river Rhine.

After VE-Day, the 406th remained in Germany for duty with the occupying forces, being transferred from the 9th Air Force to USAFE on 2 December 1945.

Squadrons and codes:	512th FS [L3]		
	513th FS [4P]		
	514th FS [O7]		
Bases:	Ashford	5.4.44	
	Tour-en-Bessin (F)	7.44	
	Cretteville (F)	17.8.44	
	Le Mans (F) (HQ only)	4.9.44	
	St. Leonard (F) (not HQ)	4.9.44	
	Mourmelon-le-Grand (F)	22.9.44	
	Metz (F)	2.2.45	
	Asch (B)	8.2.45	
	Munster/Handorf (G)	15.4.45	
	Nordholz (G)	5.6.45	→
Commanding Officers:	Col. Anthony V. Grossetta		
	Lt. Col. Converse B. Kelly	6.45	
	Lt. Col. Robert C. Brown	27.9.45	→
Aircraft:	P-47		

Squadron markings: 512th FS: Yellow noseband, later cowling, and blue/red/yellow horizontal bands across fin and rudder
513th FS: red noseband, later cowling, and blue/red/yellow horizontal bands across fin and rudder
514th FS: Blue noseband, later cowling, and blue/red/yellow horizontal bands across fin and rudder

At Ashford ALG a 406th FG P-47 stands ready for the next mission [via H. Holmes]

409th BOMBARDMENT GROUP

After arriving in England in March 1944, the 409th BG's A-20s began their part in the war on 13 April by bombing coastal gun batteries, V-weapon launching sites, airfields and other strategic targets in France in preparation for the forthcoming invasion. It was during such an attack on Amiens rail yards on 27 May that the Group suffered its first heavy losses. During the period just after D-Day, the 409th gave support to the ground forces by attacking defences, lines of communication and transport routes, and in July aided the offensive at Caen and St. Lo.

With the Allied forces well established, the 409th BG moved its base to France in September 1944 to support the advance of the 3rd Army. In December 1944 the Group converted to the A-26 aircraft, with which it took part in the Battle of the Bulge, and operated against targets in Germany until its final mission on 3 May 1945, an attack on an ammunition dump in Czechoslovakia. The Group's return to the USA began in June, its A-26s being sent to the Far East for use in the continuing war effort there.

Squadrons and codes:	640th BS [W5]			**Group marking:** Yellow band along trailing edge of rudder
	641st BS [7G]			
	642nd BS [D6]			
	643rd BS [5I]			
Bases:	Little Walden	7.3.44		
	Bretigny (F)	18.9.44		
	Laon/Couvron (F)	12.2.45	—25.6.45	
Commanding Officers:	Col. Preston J. Pender			
	Col. Thomas R. Ford	4.7.44	—25.6.45	
Aircraft:	A-20 (3.44—12.44); A-26 (12.44—6.45)			

Seen somewhat the worse for wear in France on 27 December 1944 is this A-20 of the 410th BG

[Merle Olmsted]

The 410th BG arrived in England in March/April 1944 after a period of training on A-20s in the United States, but moved base after two weeks before beginning operations in May. Like so many 9th AF light bomber Groups, the 410th spent a month of participation in the 'softening-up' process in Normandy and on D-Day bombed enemy defences and railway yards.

In July the 410th aided the ground forces in the dramatic breakthrough at St. Lo and at Caen, and in August and September switched its attention to the port of Brest and associated lines of communication. The Group moved to France in September and until mid-December attacked strategic targets to

support the Allied advance across France. Then, around Christmas, the 410th played its part in the Ardennes counter-offensive, for which it received a DUC in recognition of its bombing technique.

During several night-time operations in February 1945, the 410th used B-26s to drop flares, A-26s for target marking and its original A-20s to drop the bomb loads. For the remainder of the war, the Group continued to fly support and interdiction missions, finally converting onto A-26 aircraft but not using them operationally. After VE-Day, the 410th BG returned to the USA between June and August 1945 to be inactivated.

The black and white fin markings and code 7X identify this A-20 of the 410th BG's 645th BS   [R. Mynn]

Squadrons and bases:	644th BS [5D]	**Group marking:** Black and white		
	645th BS [7X]	band along trailing edge of		
	646th BS [8U]	rudder; coloured engine cow-		
	647th BS [6Q]	lings		
Bases:	Birch		4.4.44	
	Gosfield		16.4.44	
	Coulommiers (F)		27.9.44	
	Juvincourt (F)		9.2.45	
	Beaumont-sur-Oise (F)		22.5.45	—25.6.45
Commanding Officers:	Col. Ralph Rhudy			
	Col. Sherman R. Beaty		3.7.44	
	Col. Robert J. Hughes		12.44	—6.45
Aircraft:	A-20 (4.44—5.45); A-26 (5.45—6.45)			

416th BOMBARDMENT GROUP

After arriving in England in January and February 1944, the 416th's A-2Os entered combat in March, although holding only 55 serviceable aircrait out of an allocation of 126, and for some weeks concentrated on attacking V.1 sites in the Pas de Calais area and elsewhere. Subsequently operations against coastal defences and airfields in northern France were carried out until D-Day, when railway yards, roads and bridges were attacked in the general effort to eliminate enemy lines of supply and communication.

Later in the summer of 1944, the 416th assisted in the breakthrough at St. Lo in July and in spite of heavy resistance was able to earn a DUC for its efforts in hindering the enemy's retreat through the Falaise Gap early in August. Soon after moving to France in September, the Group raided Brest docks and radar station, and took part in the airborne attack on Holland. Support for the Allied attack on the Siegfried Line followed, before the Group converted to the A-26 aircraft during November 1944. With the new aircraft, attacks were made on lines of communication, troop movements and defended points during the Battle of the Bulge at the end of the year, and the 416th BG continued to strike strategic targets in Germany until the end of hostilities, including attacks on flak positions during the crossing of the river Rhine.

The 416th returned to the United States between July and October 1945 to be inactivated, its A-26s quickly being shipped to the Far East for possible further use.

Squadrons and codes:	668th BS [5H]	**Group marking:** White band along		
	669th BS [2A]	trailing edge of rudder;		
	670th BS [F6]	coloured propellor bosses		
	671st BS [5C]			
Bases:	Wethersfield		1.2.44	
	Melun/Villaroche (F)		21.9.44	
	Laon/Athies (F)		10.2.45	
	Cormeilles-en-Vexin (F)		25.5.45	
	Laon/Athies (F)		27.7.45	—13.9.45
Commanding Officers:	Col. Harold L. Mace			
	Col. Theodore R. Aylesworth		3.8.44	
Aircraft:	A-20 (1.44—11.44); A-26 (11.44—7.45)			

A-20J 39914 of 416th BG undergoing routine maintenance   [Merle Olmsted].

One of the first troop carrier Groups to come to England, the 434th TCG arrived in October 1943 and began a training period which continued to the invasion of France on 6 June 1944, its Army partner being the 101st Airborne Division. On D-Day the 434th towed 52 CG-4 and 32 Horsa gliders to Normandy in two operations, 'Chicago' and 'Detroit', and followed up with fifty replenishment sorties the following day. For these missions the Group received a DUC and the Croix de Guerre with Palms. In July the Group assisted the St. Lo breakthrough by supplying troop reinforcements.

During the airborne assault on Holland between 17 and 25 September 1944 the 434th dropped paratroops and towed 161 troop-carrying gliders in all, on two days. In December 1944, during the German counter-offensive in the Ardennes, the Group dropped much-needed paratroop reinforcements. A move to France in February 1945 enabled the 434th TCG to take part in the Rhine crossing operation on 24 March.

Apart from the specific operations in which the 434th took part, the Group's C-47s spent much time in transporting supplies of all sorts from England to the Continent and wounded personnel in the opposite direction. After VE-Day, the Group concentrated on carrying fuel to the Allied forces in Germany and prisoners of war to centres in France and Holland before returning home in July and August 1945.

Squadrons and codes:	71st TCS [CJ]		
	72nd TCS [CU]		
	73rd TCS [CN]		
	74th TCS [ID]		
Bases:	Fulbeck	7.10.43	
	Welford	10.12.43	
	Fulbeck	10.1.44	
	Aldermaston	3.3.44	
	Mourmelon-le-Grand (F)	2.45	—24.7.45
Commanding Officers:	Lt. Col. Fred D. Stevers		
	Col. William B. Whitacre	29.11.43	
	Lt. Col. Ben A. Garland	17.12.44	—N/K
Aircraft:	C-47; C-53; CG-4; Horsa		

Seen here at the end of December 1944 is a C-47A of the 434th TCG, 224051 [CN:N] dropping supplies to US troops under siege at Bastogne during the Ardennes counter-offensive [D. Benfield]

435th TROOP CARRIER GROUP

Another early arrival, the 435th TCG settled in England in October 1943 and began a long period of training. Large-scale glider-towing and navigation exercises formed a major part of the training programme, and towing by night was also practiced. Mass cast-offs of gliders and their landing at Welford, the 435th's base, was another function successfully carried out during this period.

Training completed, the Group dropped paratroops of the 101st AD near Cherbourg on D-Day, and later the same day and next day towed 12 CG-4 and 38 Horsa gliders carrying reinforcements to the same area. For these operations the 435th was awarded a DUC.

With the Normandy beachhead established, the 435th began a period of transporting supplies such as radar sets, clothing, rations, blood and ammunition to the Allied forces, but sent a detachment to Italy in July 1944 to take part in Operation 'Anvil', the invasion of southern France. The detachment dropped paratroops into the invasion area on 15 August and towed supply-carrying gliders next day, and also carried out general transportation missions before returning to England at the end of August.

In September 1944 the 435th TCG took part in the air attack on Holland, dropping paratroops of the 82nd and 101st ADs and towing 121 gliders carrying reinforcements. After a further period of freighting work, the Group moved to France in February 1945 to participate in the crossing of the Rhine on 24 March, in which each of the 72 C-47s towed two CG-4 gliders.

During the final week of the war, the 435th carried supplies to Allied troops in Germany and after VE-Day evacuated prisoners of war, before leaving for the USA at the end of June 1945.

Squadrons and codes:	75th TCS [SH]		
	76th TCS [CW]		
	77th TCS [IB]		
	78th TCS [CM]		
Bases:	Langar	3.11.43	
	Welford*	25.1.44	
	Bretigny (F)	13.2.45	—25.6.45
Commanding Officer:	Col. Frank J. MacNess		
Aircraft:	C-47; C-53; CG-4; Horsa		
	*detachment to Tarquinia, Italy, 20.7.44—23.8.44		

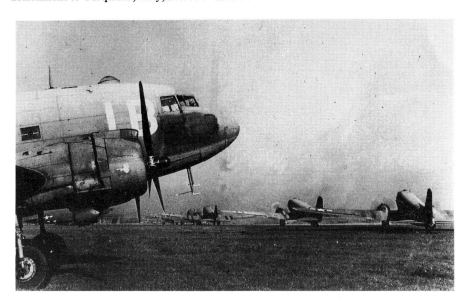

C-47s of the 435th TCG's 77th TCS at Brussels   [R. C. Sturtivant]

436th TROOP CARRIER GROUP

The 436th TCG arrived in England in January 1944 and continued its training programme for the next few months, culminating in playing its part in the D-Day operation. Early on the morning of 6 June 1944, 90 of the Group's C-47s dropped paratroops of the 82nd Airborne Division over the Normandy beachhead, and later that day towed 48 Horsa gliders carrying field artillery reinforcements to the same area. For these efforts the 436th received a DUC.

With the Allied troops established in Normandy, the 436th was able to send a detachment of aircraft and crews to Italy in July to participate in the invasion of southern France. The operation took place on 15 August, when the Group towed troop-carrying gliders and dropped paratroops, later flying re-supply sorties. After dropping supplies to Allied forces in other parts of Italy, the 436th TCG returned to England late in August

In September 1944 the Group dropped paratroops of the 101st AD over Holland and towed 207 CG-4 gliders carrying reinforcements to the same area. Between its four major operations the 436th flew many transport sorties in which urgent supplies of fuel, ammunition, food and medical equipment were carried, and on the return journeys casualties were brought back to England for hospitalisation.

Following its move to France in February 1945, the 436th's 72 C-47s each towed two CG-4 troop-carrying gliders to Wesel on 24 March for the airborne assault across the Rhine, and afterwards transported fuel to the front line and evacuated casualties. Then came VE-Day, and the 436th spent some time in carrying released prisoners and flying practice missions with the French Army before returning home in August 1945.

Squadrons and codes:	79th TCS [S6]		
	80th TCS [7D]		
	81st TCS [U5]		
	82nd TCS [3D]		
Bases:	Bottesford	6.1.44	
	Membury*	3.3.44	
	Melun/Villaroche (F)	26.2.45	—7.45
Commanding Officer:	Col. Adriel N. Williams		
Aircraft:	C-47; CG-4		
	*detachment to Voltone, Italy, 20.7.44—23.8.44		

'Damn Yankees' of the 436th TCG's 82nd TCS receiving attention
[Lawrence Riordan]

437th TROOP CARRIER GROUP

C-47s and CG-4s of the 84th TCS, 437th TCG, lined up at Coulommiers, France, ready for the Rhine crossing operation, March 1945   [D. Benfield]

After arriving in England in January 1944, the 437th TCG played its part in the Normandy campaign by towing 60 CG-4 and 18 Horsa gliders to the Cherbourg area in two operations on D-Day, followed closely by fifty re-supply sorties for the 82nd Airborne Division. For its actions on D-Day and D+1 the Group was awarded a DUC.

With other TCGs of the 9th Air Force, the 437th sent a detachment to Italy to take part on 15 August in the invasion of southern France. Re-supply sorties were flown next day, with some general transportation flights in the area, before the detachment returned to England on 24 August. The next operation was the assault on Holland over the period from 17 to 25 September 1944, during which the 437th TCG towed 140 CG-4 troop-carrying gliders and flew several reinforcing misions carrying troops and equipment. During this operation, 'Market Garden', six of the Group's C-47s were shot down, with heavy loss of life.

With the crossing of the river Rhine in prospect, the 437th moved to France in February 1945. During this operation, on 24 March, each of 80 C-47s towed two gliders to release at Wesel. Many supply flights were operated during March and April carrying much-needed material to the Armies during their rapid advance across Germany and returning with casualties and released prisoners. After VE-Day, the Group remained in France until August 1945 to transport displaced persons and homebound ex-prisoners.

Squadrons and codes:	83rd TCS [T2]		
	84th TCS [Z8]		
	85th TCS [9O]		
	86th TCS [5K]		
Bases:	Balderton	20.1.44	
	Ramsbury*	5.2.44	
	Coulommiers/Voisins (F)	25.2.45	—7.45
Commanding Officers:	Col. Cedric E. Hudgens		
	Col. Donald J. French	12.6.44	—N/K
Aircraft:	C-47; C-53; CG-4		
	*detachment to Montala, Italy, 19.7.44—23.8.44		

438th TROOP CARRIER GROUP

The 438th TCG arrived in England in February 1944 and continued its training programme, which culminated in towing 50 CG-4 and Horsa gliders carrying troops of the 82nd AD during the invasion of Normandy on 6 June 1944, for which the Group was designated as the lead element and received a DUC.

A detachment of three of the four squadrons was sent to Italy in July to take part in the invasion of southern France on 15 August by towing gliders and dropping paratroops. The detachment returned to England later in the month, the fourth squadron having operated from Welford in the meantime.

In September 1944 the 438th TCG helped the Third Army in its advance across France by dropping urgent supplies, and did the same during the airborne invasion of Holland, Operation 'Market Garden', when 198 CG-4 gliders were towed to the Eindhoven/Nijmegen area. Similar operations were flown during the Battle of the Bulge in the Ardennes at the end of December 1944. The 438th moved to France in February 1945 to take part in the crossing of the Rhine in March, the Group's final operation in the ETO. Subsequently, the 438th's C-47s evacuated Allied prisoners before returning home in August and September 1945.

Paratroops about to board C-47A 315306
of the 438th TCG's 88th TCS
[Leon Armer via D. Benfield]

Squadrons and codes:	87th TCS [3X]		
	88th TCS [M2]		
	89th TCS [4U]		
	90th TCS [Q7]		
Bases:	Welford (squadrons at Langar)	2.44	
	Greenham Common*	16.3.44	
	Prosnes (F)	2.45	
	Amiens/Glisy (F)	5.45	—8.45
Commanding Officers:	Col. John M. Donalson		
	Col. Lucien N. Powell	27.12.44	—N/K
Aircraft:	C-47; CG-4		
	*detachment at Canino, Italy, 20.7.44 23.8.44		

A Horsa glider being towed off by C-47 coded 4U:H of the 89th TCS at Greenham Common on D-Day [IWM neg. EA25878]

439th TROOP CARRIER GROUP

At Balderton on 17 September 1944 thirty of the 439th TCG's C-47s are seen being loaded with 388 paratroops to be dropped on DZ 'N' at Groesbeek, Holland. The aircraft at left is 315159 [D8:Z] 'The Argonia'
[Col. Young via D. Benfield]

The 439th TCG arrived in England, like many of its contemporaries, in February/March 1944 and went into battle on D-Day by carrying paratroops of the 101st Airborne Division in 81 aircraft to Normandy. Next day the Group's C-47s towed twenty CG-4 and thirty Horsa gliders carrying reinforcements to the beachheads and for this operation received a DUC and a French citation.

After the invasion the 439th acted as a general transport unit within the UK until a detachment was sent to Italy in July 1944 to carry out similar work and to evacuate wounded soldiers. On 15 August the Group took part in the invasion of southern France by dropping paratroops of the 517th Parachute Infantry Regt. and then towed supply-carrying gliders, these operations earning a further citation from the French.

The detachment returned to England on 25 August 1944 to resume cargo-carrying tasks but moved to France in September to take part in the Allied advance. The Group played its part in the airborne assault on Holland later in September by towing a total of 100 CG-4 gliders and dropping troops of the 82nd Airborne Division near Nijmegen. During the winter of 1944/45 the 439th's C-47s were involved in the Battle of the Bulge by hauling supply-carrying gliders to Bastogne. Two gliders were towed by each of the 72 C-47s when the 17th Airborne Division made its airborne crossing of the Rhine to land near Wesel on 24 March 1945.

Subsequently, the 439th TCG was employed in an intensive transport operation, carrying supplies of all types to the battle areas and evacuating wounded personnel. The trusty C-47s were replaced by C-46s in April 1945 and these were used to carry refugees from Germany to France and Belgium after VE-Day. The 439th, its task completed, returned home to the USA in July 1945.

Squadrons and codes:	91st TCS [L4]		
	92nd TCS [J8]		
	93rd TCS [3B]		
	94th TCS [D8]		
Bases:	Balderton	21.2.44	
	Upottery*	26.4.44	
	Juvincourt (F)	8.9.44	
	Lonray (F)	28.9.44	
	Chateaudun (F)	4.11.44	—11.7.45
Commanding Officer:	Col. Charles H. Young		
Aircraft:	C-47, C-53 (2.44—4.45); C-46 (4.45—7.45)		

*91st, 92nd and 94th TCS detached to Orbetello, Italy, 18.7.44—24.8.44; 93rd TCS operated from Ramsbury 7.8.44—16.8.44 and from Membury 16.8.44—22.8.44

Ready at Chateaudun for the Rhine crossing are the 72 C-47s and 144 CG-4A gliders of the 439th TCG. Note that the gliders are also coded L4   [D. Benfield]

440th TROOP CARRIER GROUP

After the usual period of training, the 440th TCG, which had arrived in England in March 1944, entered the fray by dropping troops of the 101st Airborne Division near Carentan in Normandy on D-Day, losing three aircraft in the process. Vital supplies were carried to the same area next day, and a DUC was awarded to the Group for its efforts. For the next few weeks the 440th flew re-supply missions, and a detachment was sent to Italy in July to carry out similar work. While there, the detachment took part in the invasion of southern France by dropping paratroops near Le Muy on 15 August and later by hauling gliders carrying reinforcements.

That part of the Group remaining in England meanwhile continued a general cargo operation, including a mission in which supplies were dropped to an infantry battalion under siege in northern France on 10 August. The Group came together again on 25 August and moved to France in September.

Paratroops of the 82nd AD were carried by the 440th and dropped near Groesbeek on 17 September during the attack on Holland, and 168 CG-4 gliders carrying reinforcements were towed to that area during the following few days. The Group's part in the Battle of the Bulge consisted of hauling supply carrying gliders for the encircled 101st AD at Bastogne on Boxing

Day 1944.

In March 1945 the 440th TCG towed 90 CG-4s carrying 17th AD troops to Wesel during the crossing of the Rhine. This was the Group's final operation, after which it was engaged in carrying supplies to the front line and evacuating casualties until VE-Day, 8 May 1945. Freed prisoners and displaced persons then became the 440th's passengers until the Group disbanded in October 1945.

Squadrons and codes:	95th TCS [9X]		
	96th TCS [6Z]		
	97th TCS [W6]		
	98th TCS [8Y]		
Bases:	Bottesford	11.3.44	
	Exeter*	18.4.44	
	Reims (F)	11.9.44	
	Le Mans (F)	30.9.44	
	Orleans (F)	2.11.44	—18.10.45
Commanding Officers:	Lt. Col. Frank X. Krebs		
	Lt. Col. Loyd C. Waldorf	18.9.44	
	Col. Frank X. Krebs	29.10.44-	—N/K
Aircraft:	C-47; CG-4		

*95th, 96th and 97th TCS detached to Ombrone, Italy, 18.7.44—24.8.44; 98th TCS operated from Ramsbury 7.8.44—23.8.44

This interesting picture, taken at Exeter in 1944, shows 440th TCG C-47s of the 98th TCS, coded 8Y; 95th TCS, coded 9X; and 96th TCS, coded 6Z. Also seen are an RAF Dakota, a UC-78, a Tiger Moth, and, in the background, a Lancaster, a C-47 minus tailplane and an Oxford [Smithsonian Institute]

441st TROOP CARRIER GROUP

Following arrival in England in March 1944, the 441st TCG began general transport duties within the UK and continued training for the forthcoming invasion of Europe. On D-Day the Group carried paratroops of the 101st Airborne Division to the Cherbourg area and next day towed fifty CG-4 gliders carrying reinforcements for the 82nd Airborne Division. A DUC was awarded to the Group for these operations.

The 441st then reverted to general cargo-carrying work, but sent a detachment to Italy in July 1944 to carry out scheduled flights between Rome and Grosseto. In August the invasion of southern France was made, and the 441st TCG took part on 15 August by dropping paratroops of the 109th Parachute Infantry Regt. and then towing reinforcement-carrying gliders. The detachment returned to England on 25 August and once more resumed general transport work.

In September 1944 the 441st TCG moved to France to participate in further operations. First came the air assault on Holland, during which the Group dropped paratroops of the 82nd and 101st Airborne Divisions near Nijmegen on 17 September and towed 168 gliders carrying reinforcements on subsequent days. The 101st AD, surrounded at Bastogne over Christmas 1944, were no doubt very pleased to see the 441st again when the Group dropped much-needed supplies.

The final big air operation of the war was the crossing of the Rhine, and the 441st played its part by hauling 96 gliders carrying the 17th Airborne Division from Dreux and Chartres to Wesel on 24 March 1945. When the armies were established east of the Rhine, the 441st carried fuel and other supplies to them, and evacuated the wounded and released PoWs until VE-Day.

After the end of hostilities the 441st TCC remained in Europe up to and beyond the inactivation of the 9th Air Force in December 1945.

Squadrons and codes:	99th TCS [3J] (to 27th ATG, 8th AF, 27.8.45)	
	100th TCS [8C]	
	301st TCS [Z4] (to 442nd TCG 18.4.45, returned 8.45)	
	302nd TCS [2L] (to 314th TCG 15.5.45)	
Bases:	Langar	17.3.44
	Merryfield*	25.4.44
	Villeneuve/Vertus (F)	8.9.44
	St. Marceau (F)	2.10.44
	Dreux (F)*	3.11.44
	Frankfurt (G) (not 301st TCS)	12.8.45
Commanding Officers:	Col. Theodore G. Kershaw	
	Col. William H. Parkhill	24.11.44
Aircraft:	C-47; C-53; CG-4	

*99th, 100th and 302nd TCS detached to Grosseto, Italy, 18.7.44—24.8.44; 301st TCS operated from Ramsbury 7.8.44—24.8.44, from St. Andre-de-l'Eure (F) 20.5.45—28.6.45, from Halle (G) 28.6.45—4.7.45 and from Berlin/Templehof (G) 4.7.45 on.

442nd TROOP CARRIER GROUP

The 442nd TCG arrived in England in March 1944 and continued its training programme prior to the invasion of Europe. Paratroops carried by the Group were dropped from 45 aircraft at St. Mere Eglise on D-Day and 56 re-supply sorties were flown next day, a DUC being awarded for the Group's efforts. A period of general cargo flying followed, but a detachment was sent to Italy in July 1944 to take part in the invasion of southern France on 15 August by towing gliders and dropping troops in the battle area.

At the end of August the detachment returned to England and the Group took part in the assault on Holland in September by towing 161 CG-4 troop carrying gliders. Another period of general cargo transport work followed, until in March 1945 the 442nd participated in the airborne crossing of the Rhine by hauling 48 CG-4s. This was the Group's final major operation, but intensive flying continued, as the 442nd was employed in evacuating released prisoners after VE-Day.

The 442nd was one of the TCGs which remained in Germany for some time after the end of the war, being transferred to USAFE on the inactivation of the 9th Air Force in December 1945.

Squadrons and codes:	303rd TCS [J7]		
	304th TCS [V4]		
	305th TCS [4J]		
	306th TCS [7H]		
Bases:	Fulbeck	29.3.44	
	Weston Zoyland*	12.6.44	
	Peray (F)	5.10.44	
	St. Andre-de-l'Eure (F)*	6.11.44	
	Munich/Riem (G)	11.9.45	→
Commanding Officers:	Col. Charles M. Smith		
	Col. John C. Kilborn	25.9.45	
	Lt. Col. Paul A. Jones	4.10.45	→
Aircraft: C-47; C-53; CG-4			

*303rd, 304th and 305th TCS were detached to Follonica (I) 18.7.44—25.8.44; 306th TCS operated from Ramsbury 7.8.44—24.8.44; all squadrons operated from Metz (F) 5.45—10.9.45.

After the dust of war had settled. C-47s of the 442nd TCG's 305th TCS on the apron at Berlin/Templehof.   [Hulton-Deutsch collection]

474th FIGHTER GROUP

About to touch down on a German airstrip on 4 October 1945 is this P38 of the 474th FG. Note the 'home-made' control tower   [Merle Olmstead]

The recently-activated 474th FG, equipped with P-38s, arrived in England in March 1944 and flew its first combat sorties, patrols over the French coast, on 25 April. Then came a period of intense activity over northern France, during which the Group attacked railway targets and bridges and during the crossing of the Channel on the night of 5/6 June 1944 the 474th provided cover. On the big day itself the Group flew many bombing sorties in support of the ground troops, and then began armed reconnaissance missions. In addition, many attacks were made on roads and troop concentrations to assist the Allied breakthrough at St. Lo.

In August 1944 the 474th FG moved to France, and one of the Group's first missions from its new ALG was an attack on retreating enemy troops in the Falaise/Argentan area on 23 August. While carrying out this operation, pilots of the 474th found large amounts of German equipment stored along the river Seine. Despite heavy opposition, the 474th's P-38s were able to destroy a large part of this equipment and associated transport, for which the Group was awarded a DUC.

Apart from a sustained campaign of strafing airfields, railway yards, bridges, roads, fuel, ammunition dumps and gun batteries, the 474th FG then carried out some escort work with bombers which were raiding strategic targets. Other targets for the 474th were gun positions near Eindhoven just before the airborne assault on Holland in September; troop concentrations in the Ardennes in December and in January 1945; and defences along the river Rhine in advance of the final major airborne operation of the war.

Operations by the 474th continued until VE-Day, and the Group returned to the USA in November 1945.

Squadrons and codes:	428th FS [F5]		
	429th FS [7Y]		
	430th FS [K6]		
Bases:	Warmwell	12.3.44	
	Neuilly (F)	6.8.44	
	St. Marceau (F)	29.8.44	
	Peronne (F)	6.9.44	
	Florennes/Juzaines (B)	1.10.44	
	Strassfeld (G)	22.3.45	
	Langensalza (G)	22.4.45	
	Schweinfurt (G)*	16.6.45	
	Stuttgart (G)	25.10.45	—21.11.45
	*430th FS at Nice (F)	15.6.45	—28.11.45
Commanding Officers:	Col. Clinton C. Wasem		
	Lt. Col. Earl C. Hedlund	17.2.45	
	Lt. Col. David L. Lewis	4.45	—N/K
Aircraft:	P-38		
Squadron markings:	428th FS:	Black triangle on tailplane; blue spinner and nose tip	
	429th FS:	Black square on tailplane; red spinner and nose tip	
	430th FS:	Black circle on tailplane; yellow spinner and nose tip	

P-38s of the 474th FG's 429th FS
[via H. Holmes]

516th TROOP CARRIER GROUP

Authorised on 12.4.45, the 516th TCG was too late to see any combat service. It appears to have comprised an amalgam of personnel and aircraft from the 31st ATG and the 27th ATG's 324th ATS, with a number of ground units.

Eventually the 516th TCG arrived in Germany, where it remained until being disbanded, but its duties during that period are unknown.

Squadrons and codes:	?	
Bases:	Grove	12.4.45
	Bovingdon	?
	(Germany)	?
Commanding Officers:	?	
Aircraft:	?	

PROVISIONAL RECONNAISSANCE GROUP

Formed in October 1944, the Provisional Reconnaissance Group absorbed three squadrons from other Groups: the 34th PRS from the 10th PRG; the 111th TRS from the 12th Air Force; and the 162nd TRS from the 363rd TRG. In March 1945, however, the Group was taken over by the newly-arrived 69th TRG, apart from the 162nd TRS, which became part of the 10th PRG.

Another P-47 of the 358th FG came to grief on a wire-mesh airstrip

A B-26 of the 454th BS, 296200 [RJ:M] lets go its bomb-load [IWM neg. EA26501]

CHAPTER 5: THE INDEPENDENT SQUADRONS

1st PATHFINDER SQUADRON (Provisional)

During the winter of 1943/44 the number of 9th Air Force bombing missions which had to be aborted due to bad weather increased significantly, many of the aircraft arriving over enemy territory to find that the cloud cover would prevent the targets being located. The overall effect was a slow-down in the Allied softening-up programme leading up to the invasion of Europe.

Obviously this state of affairs could not continue, and the decision was taken to form a specialist pathfinder squadron to lead the Bomb Groups. American-made examples of 'Oboe' navigation equipment began to arrive in December 1943 for installation in B-26s, and in February 1944 the 1st Pathfinder Squadron (Provisional) was activated. The first fifteen crews, all highly experienced men, were drawn from the then five B-26 Groups, and on 21 February the new squadron carried out its first task, when it led seventeen B-26s of the 322nd BG on a raid on Cox-

yde airfield in Belgium. By the end of that month the 1st PFS had eleven aircraft and 345 personnel.

After a couple of indifferent results, successes began to mount, and by April the enemy had realised that a specialist pathfinder unit was operating. The lead aircraft then became the target for heavy anti-aircraft fire, and on 18 April two of the B-26s were damaged in this way. However, pathfinder-led missions were now becoming the routine, and on D-Day the 1st PFS led six missions against vital targets in Normandy. The impetus was kept up over the following months, during which the squadron moved from England to France to be nearer the Bomb Group targets. After taking part in every significant operation and moving into Holland, the 1st PFS was de-activated during April 1945.

Code:	IH		
Bases:	Andrews Field	16.2.44	
	Beauvais/Tille (F)	24.9.44	
	Peronne (F)	by 1.45	
	Venlo (H)		—4.45
Commanding Officers:	Maj. (later Lt. Col.) Robert A. Porter	16.2.44	—1.11.44
	Lt. Col. William Hale	1.11.44	—N/K
Aircraft:	B-26		

14th LIAISON SQUADRON

After a trouble-free Atlantic crossing, the 14th LS arrived at its domestic accommodation at Alderley Edge, Cheshire, on 9 April 1944 and was assigned to the 9th Air Force on the following day. The arrival of a few L-5s on 15 April enabled courier missions to be started from nearby RAF Cranage on behalf of the US Third Army, which had its HQ at Peover Hall, Knutsford, under the command of Lt. Gen. George S. Patton, although the squadron's administrative assignment was to XIX TAC.

On 11 May the squadron moved to Knutsford but continued to fly its ever increasing complement of L-5s from Cranage. Two UC-78s joined the squadron at this time to augment the fleet with a faster and more powerful aircraft. During May, Flights were detached to carry out liaison duties with the US 5th Armoured Division near Marlborough in Wiltshire.

Then came D-Day, and, in readiness for the part it would play, the 14th LS sent an advance party to Ibsley on 18 June, the rest of the squadron following on 29 June. On 4 July, a significant date in American eyes, the squadron began to move to Southampton, minus aircraft, to board a LST for the Channel crossing. The LST arrived on Utah beach next day and the

squadron personnel made their way to Nehou, where the L-5s and UC-78s arrived on 11 July.

Taking up its task of acting as courier to the US Third Army, the 14th LS began a series of frequent moves from one airstrip to another as the front line advanced. During its first month in France, 67 sorties, on average, were flown each day.

On 15 November 1944 the 14th LS was affiliated to 12th Army Group for operations, but poor weather in October and November was an added obstacle to the squadron. However, it performed its task more than adequately, and included the transport of urgent medical supplies to troops beleaguered on the east bank of the river Moselle. In January 1945 the weather became even worse, and flying was badly affected. Conditions did not improve until March, when there was a big increase in the number of sorties flown. In April some unusual missions included the delivery of maps to forward troop formations and escort duty to a convoy carrying gold to Frankfurt.

After VE-Day, 8 May 1945, the 14th LS was based in Germany as part of the forces of occupation, transferring from 12th Army Group back to Third Army control on 26 July under XII TAC administration.

Code:	9S, 6C		
Bases:	Alderley Edge (domestic)	9.4.44	
	Cranage	4.44	
	Knutsford (domestic)	11.5.44	
	Ibsley	29.6.44	
	Nehou (F)	6.7.44	
	Le Repos (F)	2.8.44	
	Beauchamp (F)	4.8.44	
	Poilley (F)	7.8.44	
	St. Germain (F)	12.8.44	
	La Bozoge (F)	15.8.44	
	Dampierre (F)	20.8.44	
	Courcy (F)	25.8.44	
	St. Maurice-aux-Riches-Hommes (F)	30.8.44	
	Marson (F)	4.9.44	
	Gussainville (F)	14.9.44	
	Nancy (F)	12.10.44	
	Sandweiler (L)	31.12.44	
	Oberstein (G)	27.3.45	
	Berkersheim (G)	3.4.45	
	Hersfeld (G)	11.4.45	
	Erlangen (G)	22.4.45	
	Regensberg (G)	2.5.45	
	Holzkirchen (G)	23.5.45	
	Bamberg (G)	10.7.45	—N/K
Aircraft:	L-5 (32); UC-78 (2)		

47th LIAISON SQUADRON

Although the 47th LS travelled from the USA to England in company with the 14th LS, the two squadrons parted company at Liverpool, the 47th travelling to Cheltenham, where accommodation was found at Camp 'G'.

Practice flying on ten L-5s began on 18 April at RAF Stoke Orchard, and the squadron was allocated to the US First Army Group for operations and to IX TAC for administration. The stay at Cheltenham was short, as the squadron moved on 25 April to Heston, just west of London. 26 L-5s and two UC-78s had been taken on charge by 5 May, and the 47th LS became fully operational on 10 May. Courier services now began on routes from Heston to US Third Army HQ at Knutsford, HQ Communications Zone at Cheltenham, HQ US First Army at Bristol (using Beggars Bush Field as the airstrip) and to various units in the Plymouth area. Other tasks carried out by the 47th LS included the transportation of senior officers and some air to ground photography.

Six L-5s were detached on 30 May 1944 to RAF Oatlands Hill on Salisbury Plain for the task of carrying highly important operational mail. There, the detachment flew 365 sorties during June. Meanwhile, at Heston, a P-47D had arrived for the use of the squadron as a high-speed mail aircraft. When D-Day arrived, preparations began for a move to France, but it was 23

July before the 47th LS's 'A' Flight left for Colombieres in Normandy. The remainder of the ground element left Heston on 6 August. The squadron came together again on 10 August to begin an attachment to the US 12th Army Group, but 'A' Flight left on a number of attachments, not rejoining the squadron until mid-September.

Shortages of fuel and spare parts for the aircraft, compounded by bad weather, were problems faced by the 47th LS in October 1944, but a high level of activity was kept up. 'A' and 'B' Flights in turn were detached to Luxembourg for duty with the 12th Army Group's forward HQ, and it was not until late December that weather conditions began to improve. Two L-5B and an L-1C ambulance aircraft were received by the squadron in January 1945, the month in which the squadron's first fatality since leaving England occured. This was on 22 January, when an L-5 flying from Le Bourget to Verdun crashed into a hillside, killing the pilot. Mail and passenger carrying scheduled flights were the routine in February 1945, but a special commendation was given to the pilot of an L-5 which assisted a lost B-17 to find a suitable airfield on which to land on 25 February.

Moves were then made into Germany, where the 47th LS's attachment was transferred to HQ Command, ETO, on 1 August 1945 and to XII TAC on 23 November 1945.

Bases:	Cheltenham (domestic)	9.4.44	—25.4.44
	Stoke Orchard	18.4.44	
	Heston	25.4.44	
	Colombieres (F) ('A' Flight only)	23.7.44	
	St. Sauveur-Lendelin (F)	10.8.44	
	Laval (F)	21.8.44	
	Buc (F)	2.9.44	
	Verdun (F)	17.9.44	
	Ober Olm (G)		
	Langensalza (G)		
	Erfurt (G)		
	Herzogenaurach (G)		
	Wiesbaden (G)		
Aircraft:	L-5; UC-78; L-1		

72nd LIAISON SQUADRON

On 29 November 1944, the 72nd LS, then based at Epinal in France, was placed under 9th Air Force control, while remaining attached to the US Seventh Army. From 11 December the squadron worked with the 6th Army Group while still retaining allegiance to the Seventh Army, and remained fairly static for some time. Detachments were sent, however, to Nice, Marsailles, Grenoble and other locations before the squadron began a series of moves into Germany in March 1945, culminating in the squadron's transfer out of the 9th Air Force on 20 May 1945.

Bases:		
	Epinal (F)	
	Buhl (F)	1.12.44
	Epinal (F)	2.1.45
	Buhl (F)	11.3.45
	Sarreguemines (F)	22.3.45
	Kaiserslauten (G)	26.3.45
	Darmstadt (G)	1.4.45
	Kitzingen (G)	15.4.45
	Gmund (G)	27.4.45
	Augsburg (G)	2.5.45 →
Aircraft:	L-5	

112th LIAISON SQUADRON

When assigned to the 9th Air Force on 7 June 1944, the 112th LS had just arrived at Liverpool after the Atlantic crossing from New York. Next day the squadron personnel arrived at Kingston Deverill in Wiltshire, where supplies and equipment, except aircraft, were collected. On 20 June the 112th moved on, to domestic accommodation on Hurst Park racecourse, on the Surrey bank of the river Thames, and became attached to SHAEF Rear HQ at nearby Camp Griffiss, Bushy Park, where there was an airstrip.

Heston was to be the main airfield from which the 112th LS would operate, however. The first L-5s for the squadron arrived on 24 June and training and courier flights got under way, amidst a steady bombardment by V.1 flying bombs. Many of the courier flights were to Southwick Park, near Portsmouth, SHAEF's forward HQ, which was also vulnerable to V.1s. Two Flights of the 112th LS, 'A' and 'B', were put on readiness for a move to France early in July 1944, but no order was received for some time. Meanwhile, two UC-78s were taken on charge for ferrying senior officers across the Channel. It was 4 August before personnel of the two Flights left Heston for Valognes, another batch following on 22 August. The aircraft arrived safely and were based initially at Valognes and Jullouville. HQ Flight personnel were transported to Jullouville in eight C-47s on 27 August, and the squadron's work for SHAEF continued.

By late September 1944 the various Flights of the 112th LS were operating from different locations,; the HQ and 'C' and 'D' Flights were at Buc, 'A' Flight at Reims and 'B' Flight at Orly. Poor winter weather restricted operations somewhat, but conditions improved in February. Two non-standard aircraft taken on by the 112th were an L-1C equipped with a public address system and a C-47 which was allocated to HQ 21st Army Group and operated for them by the 112th LS.

By VE-Day, HQ, 'A' and 'B' Flights were at Buc, 'C' Flight was at Reims and 'D' Flight at Frankfurt-am-Main. The squadron's attachment to SHAEF ended on 21 July and to the 9th Air Force on 10 August 1945.

An L-4 as used by the independent liasion squadrons of the 9th Air Force, and by a few of the operational Groups, seen here in the snow at Rivenhall as a B-26 lands
[B. Stait]

Bases:	Kingston Deverill (domestic)	9.6.44	
	Hurst Park (domestic)	20.6.44	
	Heston *	30.6.44	
	Jullouville (F)	27.8.44	
	Buc (F) **	24.9.44	
	Frankfurt-am-Main	21.6.45	—8.45
	*detachment at Valognes (F)	6.8.44	—9.9.44
	**detachment at Namur (B)	26.10.44	—11.2.45
Aircraft:	L-5 (twenty-nine); UC-78 (2); L-1 (one); C-47 (1)		

121st LIAISON SQUADRON

Assigned to the 9th Air Force for little more than a three-week period at the end of 1944, the 121st LS was engaged in operations in support of the US Fifth Army and Sixth Army Group in the south of France.

Bases:	Vittel (F)
Aircraft:	L-4; L-5

125th LIAISON SQUADRON

After making the transatlantic journey in company with the 112th LS, the 125th arrived at Cheltenham on 9 June 1944. There equipment was issued, and ten days later the squadron moved to Chedworth airfield, where L-5 aircraft soon began to arrive.

Training in navigation procedures then started, and soon a courier service for HQ Communications Zone, located at Cheltenham, began. Chedworth proved unsatisfactory as a base, and the squadron moved to New Zealand Farm, another RAF airfield. On 29 July the 125th became attached to HQ US Ninth Army at Clifton College, Bristol, and began to use both Whitchurch airfield and Beggars Bush Field in Bristol for liaison and mail flights. Three Flights of the squadron left for France on 23 August, and squadron HQ and 'C' Flight followed soon afterwards via Utah Beach.

The 125th moved with the Ninth Army through France into Belgium and Holland and 'B' Flight carried on into Germany by mid-December. By March 1945 the whole squadron was in Germany, and made several moves forward in April, a peak month in the 125th LS's activities. Finally, the squadron was based at Frankfurt-am-Main from July 1945 until just after the 9th Air Force's inactivation in Europe in December 1945.

298681, a 9th Air Force L-5, tied down in wintry conditions somewhere near the front line [IWM neg. FRA200450]

Bases:	Cheltenham (Camp G) (domestic)	9.6.44
	Chedworth	19.6.44
	New Zealand Farm (with domestic accommodation at Erle Stoke)	9.7.44
	St. Sauver-Lendelin (F)	1.9.44
	Rennes (F)	3.9.44
	Arlon (B)	1.10.44
	Maastricht (H)	21.10.44
	Munchen-Gladbach (G)	9.3.45
	Haltern (G)	4.4.45
	Gutersloh (G)	12.4.45
	Braunschweig (G)	24.4.45
	Heidelberg (G)	10.6.45
	Frankfurt-am-Main (G)	25.7.45 →
Aircraft:	L-5	

A 125th LS L-5 about to take off from the muddy airstrip near Kornelimunster, Germany   [IWM neg. EA48915]

153rd LIAISON SQUADRON

First of the liaison squadrons to arrive in the ETO was the 153rd OS, which came to Membury in September 1942 as part of the 8th Air Force's 67th OG. Redesignation to the 153rd LS came on 12 October 1943, and in December the squadron, by now based at Keevil, became part of the 9th Air Force's IX FC. Equipped with fifteen A-20Bs, two L-4Bs and an Oxford, the 153rd was designated as a target-towing unit on 25 December, but as specialised aircraft for this function failed to arrive, squadron personnel were notified that the 153rd would revert to a liaison role, using L-4s only. The squadron's attachment to the US First Army began on 4 February 1944, and soon a move was made to New Zealand Farm airfield. However, urgent requirements for liaison aircraft to fly daily missions for First Army's Corps HQ meant that the squadron's four Flights were detached to other airstrips: 'A' Flight to Norton Manor, near Taunton; 'B' Flight to Breamore House, near Salisbury; 'C' Flight to Knook Camp, near Warminster; and 'D' Flight to First Army HQ in Bristol, using Whitchurh airfield and Beggars

Bush Field. A batch of L-5 aircraft now arrived and by March 1944 outnumbered the L-4s. Intensive flying during this period included a good deal of photographic work.

Just before D-Day, the 153rd, which had been assigned to IX TAC from 25 April, began its preparations for its part in the invasion. All the aircraft were brought back to New Zealand Farm before flying to Middle Wallop, the jumping-off point for Normandy. On 18 June the 153rd came together as one at Vouilly, from where rapid moves were made through France and into Belgium in parellel with the advance of the US First Army. From 15 November 1944 the 153rd was attached to the 12th Army Group, and early in 1945 received a few L-5B casevac aircraft. A number of the squadron's aircraft met with accidents during the months in the front line, a few of them shot down by flak or enemy aircraft.

The 153rd LS was tranaferred to XII TAC in July 1945 to work with the US Seventh Army, but was inactivated on 15 December 1945, a few days after the 9th Air Force itself.

Code:	8R	
Bases:	Keevil	
	New Zealand Farm (with domestic accommodation at Erle Stoke)	13.3.44
	Vouilly (F)	18.6.44
	Canisy (F)	6.8.44
	St. Pois (F)	11.8.44

Couterne (F)	23.8.44	
Maillebois (F)	25.8.44	
St. Cyr (F)	2.9.44	
Vuel (B)	10.9.44	
Ham (B)	12.9.44	
Stree (B)	16.9.44	
Verviers (B)	20.9.44	
Spa (B)	24.10.44	
Liege (B)	18.12.44	
Tongres (B)	23.12.44	
Spa (B)	18.1.45	
Duren (G)	9.3.45	
Euskirchen (G)	16.3.45	
Bad Godesberg (G)	30.3.45	
Marburg (G)	5.4.45	
Bad Wildungen (G)	15.4.45	
Weimar (G)	24.4.45	
Braunschweig (G)	20.5.45	
Augsburg (G)	4.6.45	
Heidelberg (G)	25.7.45	—12.45
Aircraft: A-20 (12.43—2.44); Oxford; L-4; L-5		

158th LIAISON SQUADRON

Last of the liaison squadrons to arrive in England was the 158th, which disembarked at the end of November 1944. At Camp Doddington, near Nantwich in Cheshire supplies were issued, but not aircraft. After a period of consolidation, the 158th LS left for Normandy on 21 January 1945 for attachment to the US Fifteenth Army's Twelfth Army Group.

Within a few days, the 158th received some L-5 aircraft and moved into Belgium, although Flights were detached to a number of locations. Several of the squadron's L-5s were now equipped with VHF radio for use during close support work, and two L-1Cs were attached from the Fifteenth Army, one crashing on 10 March with two fatalities. Other accidents to L-5s were often due to their use of tiny airstrips intended for the landing characteristics of L-4s.

On 17 March the 158th moved into Germany, but returned to France in July to become part of European ATS on 25 September. The squadron was still in France when the 9th Air Force was inactivated in December 1945.

Bases:	Nantwich (domestic only)	26.11.44
	Somme-Suippes (F)	4.2.45
	Celles (B)	16.2.45
	Ahrweiler (G)	17.4.45
	Orly (F)	22.7.45
	Villacoublay (F)	18.11.45
Aircraft:	L-5 (29); L-1C (2)	

167th LIAISON SQUADRON

Activated in February 1945 in France, the 167th LS was assigned at once to the 9th Air Force and attached to the 6th Army Group. The squadron's main function was initially as a courier unit, operating between 6th Army Group HQ and the front line, but on 20 May 1945, the war in Europe over, it became part of XII TAC in Germany. As such the 167th LS was still operating at the time the 9th Air Force was inactivated.

Bases:	Vittel (F)	19.2.45
	Kaiserslauten (G)	5.4.45
	Pfaffengrund (G)	14.4.45	→
Aircraft:	L-4; L-5	

173rd LIAISON SQUADRON

The first of the liaison squadrons to arrive in Europe without staging through England, the 173rd LS was activated on 24 October 1944 and assigned to the 9th Air Force on 3 November. It was attached to HQ ETOUSA and operated from Paris (Orly) on courier duties until October 1945.

Bases:	Orly (F)	24.10.44	—10.45
Aircraft:	L-4; L-5; UC-78		

422nd NIGHT FIGHTER SQUADRON

On arrival in England from Florida on 7 March 1944, the 422nd NFS found itself at the hill-top airfield of Charmy Down, near Bath. The squadron had trained to fly the P-61 Black Widow aircraft, but none were available at Charmy Down, and, as the 422nd was the first night-fighter squadron in the 9th Air Force, a good deal of confusion reigned. An Oxford and a UC-78 were provided for continuation training, and some of the pilots were sent to RAF night-fighter bases to get an idea of what was required of them. On 7 May 1944 the sqaudron moved to Scorton in Yorkshire, the northernmost 9th Air Force airfield, where the first P-61 arrived, at long last, on 23 May.

Intensive training began as soon as enough P-61s had arrived, and many affiliation practices were carried out with Halifaxes from nearby RAF Croft. At the end of June 1944, a detachment of aircraft and crews was sent to Hurn, near Bournemouth, for four weeks comparative trials with Mosquitos, in which the P-61 excelled itself in many ways. A further detachment visited Ford in Sussex on 15 July to assist in the defence against V.1 pilotless bombs, one of these machines being shot down into the English Channel.

On 30 July 1944 the 422nd NFS completed a move from England to a new base near Cherbourg in northern France, and subsequently followed the advance of the Allied forces towards Germany as part of IX ADC. In October, however, in view of the lack of 'trade' for defensive night-fighters in the area, the 422nd was transfered to IX TAC. Under this new assignment, the 422nd's P-61s were armed with rockets in addition to their 20mm cannon and were used on offensive night intruder missions as well as defensive work. During the early part of 1945 a number of A-20s were added to the squadron to carry out flare-dropping and night attack sorties.

The 422nd NFS continued to carry out its vital dual task during the final months of hostilities, the last few of which were spent in Germany.

A tight formation of P-61 night-fighters includes, centre, 25564 'Jukin Judy' with sharks-teeth and eye, and, right, 25573 with a large heart on the nose.
[Merle Olmsted]

Bases:	Charmy Down	7.3.44	
	Scorton	7.5.44	
	Maupertus (F)	25.7.44	
	Chateaudun (F)	28.8.44	
	Florennes/Juzaines (B)	16.9.44	
	Strassfeld (G)	6.4.45	
	Langensalza (G)	24.4.45	—N/K
Commanding Officers:	Lt. Col. Oris B. Johnson		
Aircraft:	P-61; A-20 (early 1945)		

425th NIGHT FIGHTER SQUADRON

The only other night-fighter squadron assigned to the 9th Air Force in the ETO, the 425th followed the 422nd to England, arriving at Charmy Down just after the 422nd had left. After less than three weeks on the hill-top airfield, the 425th moved to Scorton to join in the training programme with the 422nd, and took part in the same four-week detachment at Hurn from 28 June. Following a similar period on anti-V.1 missions, the 425th NFS moved to Vannes in France in August to follow the Allied advance.

Like the 422nd, the 425th was given night intruder work, using HVAR rockets with which the P-61s had been equipped, in October 1944. For this, the 425th was re-assigned from IX ADC to XIX TAC, with which the squadron remained for the rest of the war. A shortage of P-61s at the end of 1944 led to the use of seven Mosquito NF.XIII night-fighters which were on loan to the USAAF from the RAF at the time, and a few A-20s. With this mixed fleet, the 425th continued to follow the Allies across Europe, ending in Germany in mid-April 1945.

Bases:	Charmy Down	26.4.44	
	Scorton	12.6.44	
	Vannes (F)	18.8.44	
	?	1.9.44	
	Coulommiers	11.9.44	
	Prosnes (F)	13.10.44	
	Rouvres/Etain (F)	9.11.44	
	Frankfurt-am-Main (G)	12.4.45	
	Furth (G)	2.5.45	—N/K
Commanding Officers:	Maj. Leon G. Lewis		
Aircraft:	P-61; Mosquito (early 1945); A-20 (early 1945)		

At BAD1, Burtonwood, apparently new P-61 239730 is readied for service in 1944, resplendent in all-black finish

[Carl J. Winkleman via Aldon Ferguson]

IX AIR FORCE TROOP CARRIER COMMAND PATHFINDER SCHOOL/PATHFINDER GROUP (Prov.)

Formed in February 1944 to provide specialist pathfinder training to crews of IX TCC, the PFS originally flew seven C-47s equipped with either GEE or SCR-717 radar. Twenty crews reported for training.

To the PFS fell the honour of being the first TCC unit to depart from its English base for the D-Day operation. This was at 21.30 on D-1, when twenty of the PFS's C-47s left North Witham carrying about 200 troops whose task it would be to prepare the dropping zones for the 82nd and 101st Airborne Divisions. The PFS's part in the huge operation was highly suc-

cessful, only one aircraft being lost to enemy action.

Later, the PFS trained Polish airborne troops before being retitled Pathfinder Group (Provisional) in September 1944, and in Operation Market Garden carried troops from North Witham, although the unit had moved to Chalgrove a few days previously. Participation was also taken in the Ardennes campaign at the end of December 1944 and in the Rhine crossing in March 1945, after which the PFG (Prov.) dispersed into the TCGs from which the unit had developed.

Squadrons:	1st PF Sqdn.		
	2nd PF Sqdn.		
	3rd PF Sqdn.		
	4th PF Sqdn.		
Bases:	Cottesmore	2.44	
	North Witham	23.3.44	
	Chalgrove	13.9.44	
	Chartres (F)	5.3.45	—N/K
Commanding Officers:	Col. Joel Crouch		
Aircraft:	C-47; C-53; C-109 (four in 3.45)		

One of twenty C-47s of the Troop Carrier Command Pathfinder School with its load of paratroops on D-Day   [D. Benfield]

Other 9th Air Force units which operated aircraft in a communications or liaison role included the 9th Air Force HQ Squadron, which flew L-5s from Chedworth in the summer of 1944; IX Engineer Command, which used light aircraft in searches for airstrip sites; and some Service Groups. Details of the aircraft and the airfields they frequented are sparse; it may be, for example, that 9th Air Force HQ Squadron also used Smith's Lawn airfield in Windsor Great Park, in view of its proximity to the HQ at Ascot. Certainly L-5s and UC-78s are known to have flown from there, but whether or not they belonged to the 9th AF is not recorded. The author would very much like to receive, via the publisher, any further information on this subject.

APPENDIX A: MAPS

Map of Southern England and Wales showing location of 9th Air Force airfields and airstrips.

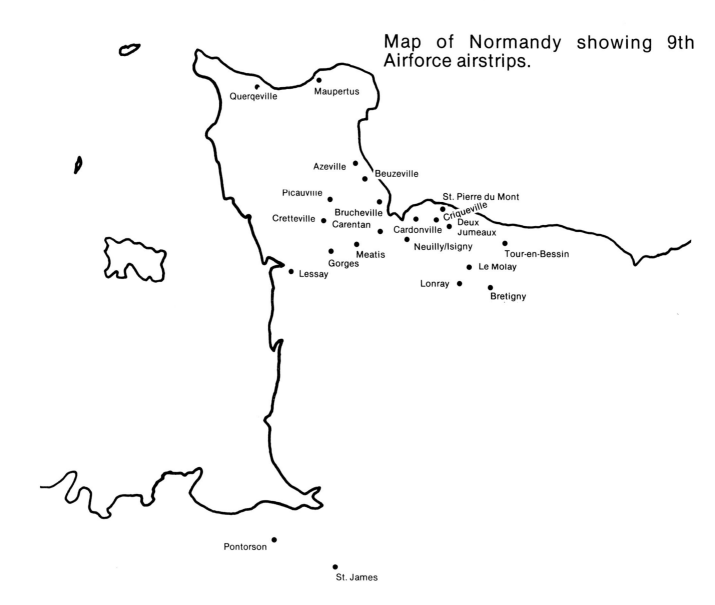

Map of Normandy showing 9th Airforce airstrips.

Querqeville
Maupertus
Azeville
Beuzeville
Picauville
St. Pierre du Mont
Brucheville
Crriqueville
Cretteville
Carentan
Cardonville
Deux Jumeaux
Neuilly/Isigny
Tour-en-Bessin
Meatis
Gorges
Le Molay
Lessay
Lonray
Bretigny
Pontorson
St. James

Ready to board: camouflaged and heavily-kitted paratroops at Upottery
[via R. C. Sturtivant]

APPENDIX B: BASES OF 9th AIR FORCE FLYING UNITS

9th AIR FORCE AIRFIELDS AND AIRSTRIPS IN THE UNITED KINGDOM

Stn. No.		
467	Aldermaston	12th TRS (1.44 — 3.44)
		15th TRS (12.43 — 3.44)
		370th FG (2.44)
		434th TCG (3.44 — 2.45)
406	Andover	370th FG (2.44 — 7.44)
485	Andrews Field★	322nd BG (to 9.44)
		1st PFS (prov.) (2.44 — 9.44)
417	Ashford (ALG)	406th FG (4.44 — 7.44)
482	Balderton	437th TCG (1.44 — 2.44)
		439th TCG (2.44 — 4.44)
483	Barkston Heath	61st TCG (2.44 — 3.45)
		349th TCG (3.45 — 4.45)
408	Beaulieu	365th FG (3.44 — 6.44)
		323rd BG (7.44 — 8.44)
149	Birch★	410th BG (4.44)
415	Bisterne (ALG)	371st FG (3.44 — 6.44)
161	Boreham★	394th BG (3.44 — 7.44)
150	Boxted★	354th FG (11.43 — 4.44)
481	Bottesford	436th TCG (1.44 — 3.44)
		440th TCG (3.44 — 4.44)
440	Breamore	'B' Flight, 153rd LS
465	Chalgrove	HQ 10th PG (2.44 — 8.44)
		33rd PRS (4.44 — 8.44)
		PFG (Prov.) (9.44 — 3.45)
487	Charmy Down	422nd NFS (3.44 — 5.44)
		425th NFS (4.44 — 6.44)
		155th PRS (4.44 — 5.44)
----	Chedworth +	125th LS (6.44 — 7.44)
404	Chilbolton	368th FG (3.44 — 6.44)
		12th TRS (3.44)
		15th TRS (3.44)
162	Chipping Ongar★	387th BG (to 7.44)
416	Christchurch	405th FG (3.44 — 6. 44)
461	Church Stanton (Culmhead)	Used in 1944 but no 9th AF units based
489	Cottesmore	316th TCG (2.44 — 5.45)
		TCC Pathfinder School (2.44 — 3.44)
----	Cranage +	14th LS (4.44 — 6.44)
458	Down Ampney	Allocated to but not used by 9th Air Force
358	Earls Colne★	323rd BG (to 7.44)
463	Exeter	440th TCG (4.44 — 9.44)
484	Folkingham	313th TCG (2.44 — 2.45)
488	Fulbeck	434th TCG (10.43 — 12.43, 1.44 — 3.44)
		442nd TCG (3.44 — 6.44)
154	Gosfield★	365th FG (12.43 — 3.44)
		397th BG (4.44)
		410th BG (4.44 — 9.44)
164	Great Dunmow★	386th BG (to 10.44)
486	Greenham Common★	354th FG (11.43)
		12th TRS (12.43 — 1.44)
		368th FG (1.44 — 3.44)
		438th TCG (3.44 — 2.45)

519	Grove*	31st ATG (11.43 — 9.44, 12.44 on)
		1st TG (Prov.) (9.44)
		516th TCG (4.45 on)
412	Headcorn (ALG)	362nd FG (4.44 — 7.44)
510	Heston +	47th LS (4.44 — 8.44)
		112th LS (6.44 — 8.44)
411	High Halden (ALG)	358th FG (4.44 — 7.44)
455	Holmsley South	394th BG (7.44 — 8.44)
492	Hurn +	397th BG (8.44)
347	Ibsley*	48th FG (3.44 — 6.44)
		371st FG det. (4.44 — 5.44)
		14th LS (6.44 — 7.44)
		367th FG (7.44)
471	Keevil*	363rd FG (12.43 — 1.44)
		153rd LS (11.43 — 3.44)
418	Kingsnorth (ALG)	36th FG (4.44 — 7.44)
----	Knook Camp, Warminster	'C' Flight, 153rd LS
490	Langar	435th TCG (11.43 — 1.44)
		438th TCG det. sqdns. (2.44 — 3.44)
		441st TCG (3.44 — 4.44)
410	Lashenden (ALG)	354th FG (4.44 — 6.44)
165	Little Walden*	409th BG (3.44 — 9.44)
551	Lymington (ALG)	50th FG (4.44 — 6.44)
166	Matching*	391st BG (1.44 — 9.44)
466	Membury*	67th RG (to 12.43)
		107th TRS (to 12.43)
		109th TRS (to 12.43)
		153rd LS (10.43 — 11.43)
		366th FG (1.44 — 3.44)
		436th TCG (3.44 — 2.45)
464	Merryfield	441st TCG (4.44 — 9.44)
449	Middle Wallop +	67th TRG (12.43 — 7.44)
		12th TRS (3.44 — 7.44)
		15th TRS (3.44 — 6.44)
		30th PRS (5.44 — 6.44)
----	New Zealand Farm +	153rd LS (3.44 — 6.44)
		125th LS (7.44 — 9.44)
479	North Witham	TCC Pathfinder School (3.44 — 9.44)
----	Norton Manor, Taunton	'A' Flight, 153rd LS
469	Ramsbury*	437th TCG (2.44 — 2.45)
157	Raydon*	357th FG (11.43 — 1.44)
		358th FG (1.44 — 4.44)
168	Rivenhall*	363rd FG (1.44 — 4.44)
		397th BG (4.44 — 8.44)
538	Saltby	314th TCG (2.44 — 3.45)
425	Scorton	422nd NFS (5.44 — 7.44)
		425th NFS (6.44 — 8.44)
----	Smith's Lawn, Windsor Gt. Park	N/K
493	Spanhoe	315th TCG (2.44 — 4.45)
169	Stansted	344th BG (2.44 — 9.44)
413	Staplehurst (ALG)	363rd FG (4.44 — 7.44)
----	Stoke Orchard +	47th LS (4.44)
452	Stoney Cross	367th FG (4.44 — 7.44)
		387th BG (7.44 — 9.44)
407	Thruxton	366th FG (3.44 — 6. 44)
462	Upottery	439th TCG (4.44 — 9.44)
454	Warmwell +	474th FG (3.44 — 8. 44)
474	Welford*	315th TCG (11.43 — 2.44)
		434th TCG (12.43 — 1.44)
		435th TCG (1.44 — 2.45)
		438th TCG (2.44 — 3.44)
447	Weston Zoyland	442nd TCG (6.44 — 10.44)
170	Wethersfield	416th BG (2.44 — 9.44)
414	Winkton (ALG)	404th FG (4.44 — 7. 44)
419	Woodchurch (ALG)	373rd FG (4.44 — 7.44)
159	Wormingford	362nd FG (11.43 — 4.44)

*signifies an airfield transferred from the 8th Air Force
+ signifies an airfield where the 9th Air Force unit was a 'lodger'

AIRFIELDS IN EUROPE ON WHICH 9th AIR FORCE FLYING UNITS WERE BASED

FRANCE

B-92	Abbeville/Drucat
B-54	Achiet
B-48	Amiens/Glisy
A-76	Athis
A-7	Azeville
	Beauchamps
A-61	Beauvais/Tille
A-60	Beaumont-sur-Oise
A-6	Beuzeville-au-Plain
A-48	Bretigny
A-16	Brucheville
Y-4	Buc
	Buhl
A-74	Cambrais/Niergnies
	Canisy
A-10	Carentan
A-3	Cardonville
	Chapelle
A-40	Chartres
A-39	Chateaudun
A-71	Clastres
	Colombieres
A-59	Cormeilles-en-Vexin
A-94	Conflans/Doncourt
A-58	Coulommiers/Voisins
	Courcy
	Couterne
A-81	Creil
A-14	Cretteville
A-2	Cricqueville-en-Bessin
	Dampierre
A-83	Denain/Prouvy
A-4	Deux Jumeaux
Y-9	Dijon/Longvic
Y-7	Dole/Tavaux
A-41	Dreux/Vermouillet
	Epinal
A-31	Gael
A-26	Gorges
	Gussainville
	Haguenau
	Jullouville
A-68	Juvincourt
	La Bozoge
A-69	Laon/Athies
A-70	Laon/Couvron
A-19	La Vielle
A-57	Laval
A-35	Le Mans
A-9	Le Molay
	Le Repas
A-20	Lessay
A-12	Lignerolles
A-45	Lonray
Y-6	Lyons/Bron
	Maillebois
	Marson
A-15	Maupertus
A-17	Meautis
Y-34	Metz/Frescaty
A-55	Melun/Villaroche
A-38	Montreuil
A-80	Mourmelon-le-Grand
Y-42	Nancy/Essey
	Nehou
A-11	Neuilly/Isigny
A-66	Orconte

A-50	Orleans/Bricy
A-47	Orly
A-44	Peray
A-72	Peronne
A-65	Perthes
A-8	Picauville
	Poilley
B-44	Poix
A-28	Pontorson
A-79	Prosnes
A-23	Querqueville
A-62	Reims/Champagne
A-27	Rennes/St. Jacques
A-98	Rosieres-en-Haye
A-82	Rouvres/Etain
A-73	Roye/Amy
B-24	St. Andre-de-l'Eure
	St. Cyr
A-64	St. Dizier
	St. Germain
A-29	St. James
A-36	St. Leonard
	St. Mere Eglise
	St. Maurice-aux-Riches-Hommes
A-43	St. Marceau
A-1	St. Pierre du Mont
	St. Pois
	St. Sauveur-Lendelin
	Sarreguemines
	Somme-Suippes
Y-1	Tantonville
A-90	Toul/Croix-de-Metz
A-13	Tour-en-Bessin
A-46	Toussus-le-Noble
	Valenciennes
	Valognes
A-33	Vannes
Y-28	Verdun/Charny
A-42	Villacoublay
A-63	Villeneuve/Vertus
	Vittel
B-50	Vitry-en-Artois
A-67	Vitry-le-Francois
	Vouilly

BELGIUM

B-70	Antwerp/Deurne
	Arlon
Y-29	Asch
	Celles
A-84	Chievres/Mons
A-87	Charleroi
A-78	Florennes/Juzaine
	Gosselies
	Ham
A-89	Le Culot
A-93	Liege/Bierset
Y-47	Namur
Y-32	Ophoven
A-92	St. Trond
	Spa
	Stree
	Tongres
	Verviers
	Vuel
	Zwartburg

HOLLAND

Y-55	Venlo
Y-44	Maastricht/Beek

LUXEMBURG

A-97	Sandweiler

AUSTRIA

R-87	Horsching
R-88	Innsbruck

GERMANY

Y-46	Aachen
	Ahrweiler
R-45	Ansbach
	Arolsen
R-84	Augsburg
	Bad Godesberg
	Bad Wildungen
	Bamberg
R-26	Bayreuth/Bindlach
	Berkersheim
	Berlin/Tempelhof
R-37	Braunschweig/Waggum
R-38	Braunschweig/Broitzen
R-42	Buchschwabach
Y-76	Darmstadt
Y-43	Duren
R-9	Erfurt/Bindersleben
R-11	Eschwege
	Euskirchen
	Frankenburg
Y-74	Frankfurt/Eschborn
Y-73	Frankfurt/Rhein Main
Y-86	Fritzlar
R-28	Furth
R-30	Furth/Industriehaven
R-77	Gablingen
Y-90	Giebelstadt
	Gmund
Y-99	Gutersloh
	Halle
	Haltern
	Haunstetten
Y-94	Handorf
	Heidelberg
	Hersfeld
R-29	Herzogenaurach
	Holzkirchen
Y-91	Hanau/Langendiebach
	Hornel
R-10	Illesheim
	Kaiserslautern

R-12	Kassel/Rothwesten
Y-54	Kelz
	Kempten
R-6	Kitzingen
R-78	Landsberg
R-2	Langensalza
R-59	Leipheim
Y-83	Limburg-am-der-Lahn
Y-98	Lippstadt
Y-79	Mannheim/Sandhofen
	Marburg
R-82	Munich/Reim
Y-56	Munchen-Gladbach
Y-94	Munster/Handorf
	Nesselwang
Y-62	Neidermennig
	Nordholz
Y-64	Ober Olm
	Oberstein
	Pffafengrund
R-66	Regensburg/Profening
R-75	Schleissheim
R-79	Schongrau
R-25	Schweinfurt
Y-59	Strassfeld
R-68	Straubing
R-50	Stuttgart/Echterdingen
Y-51	Vogelsang
	Wickenrode
R-7	Weimar
Y-80	Wiesbaden

Notes:
A signifies US usage
B signifies mainly RAF usage
Y signifies airfields taken over by US and French troops advancing from southern France
R signifies airfields in Germany occupied by USAAF

Welford airfield seen from the air on 5 March 1944, showing CG-4A gliders scattered around the airfield after a practice landing and C-47s parked in the technical area.

[via D. Benfield]

Folkingham airfield seen from the air on 9 May 1944

[via D. Benfield]

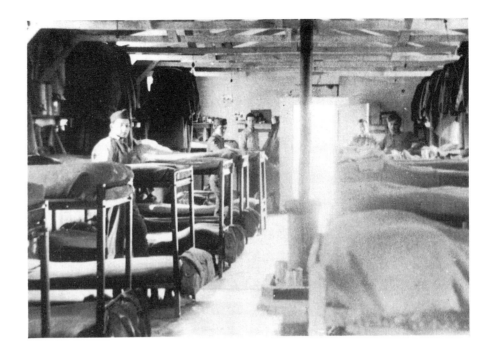

Living accommodation for Enlisted Men
at Saltby   [D. Benfield]

Folkingham control tower, with a flimsy
cabin perched on the roof, is the scene on
18 September 1944 for a final briefing of
313th TCG crews about to take part in the
assault on Holland.   [via D. Benfield]

Bearable in summer but not so good in
winter were the pyramidal tents. These
were at airstrip B.48, Amiens, France
                            [D. Benfield]

APPENDIX C: BASES OF MAJOR NON-FLYING UNITS

Minor units and locations are excluded. For locations of Wing HQs see Chapter 3 and for movements of the MR&RS see Appendix E.

Stn. No.	Location	Command	Used by
—	Alderley Edge, Cheshire		Domestic accomm. for LSs
476	Aldermaston Court, Berks.		HQ IX ASC (12.43—2.44)
			HQ XIX ASC/TAC (2.44—7.44)
402	Arborfield Cross, Berks.		
472	Ascot (Sunninghill Park), Berks.		HQ 9th AF
			HQ AFSC (10.43—8.44)
			HQ IX TCC (9.44—9.45)
544	Ashdown Park, Sussex	IX ASC	
433	Bishopstrow, Wilts.	IX AFSC	13th RCD (6.44—10.44)
436	Bois Hall, Essex	IX ADC	118th AAA Group
801	Bournemouth, Hants.	IX AFSC	HQ IX BADA
491	Bray Court, Berks.	IX EC	HQ IX EC
440	Breamore, Wilts.		40th Mobile Comms. Sqdn. (det. YA)
			21st Weather Sqdn. (det. YA)
441	Bruern Abbey, Northants.	IX EC	HQ 877th EAB
421	Chapel Row, Sussex	XXIX TAC	306th Fighter Control Sqdn.
—	Cheltenham (Camp G), Glos.		Domestic accomm. for LSs
404	Chilbolton, Hants.	IX AFSC	5th TAD and associated
			ADGs, SGs and MR&RSs
434	Chisledon, Wilts.	IX EC	EABs in training
—	Cinderford, Glos.	IX AFSC	1st AADA
423	Cokethorpe, Northants.	IX EC	926th EAR
—	Cranbrook, Kent	IX AFSC	39th Field Hospital
429	Crookham Common, Berks.	IX AFSC	Glider Assembly Depot,
			with associated MR&RSs
435	Erle Stoke, Wilts.		Domestic accomm. for LSs
548	Eccles Road	IX AFSC	1st TAD (12.44 on)
803	Filton, Bristol	IX AFSC	Aircraft Assembly Depot,
			with associated MR&RSs
—	Friston, Sussex		40th Mobile Comms. Sqdn. (det. E)
			21st Weather Sqdn. (det. E)
480	Grantham (St. Vincents), Lincs.	IX TCC	HQ IX TCC (12.43—9.44)
422	Great Barrington, Glos.	IX EC	EABs in training
519	Grove, Berks.	IX AFSC	3rd TAD and associated
			ADGs, SGs and MR&RSs
405	Hampstead, London	IX ADC	HQ IX ADC (7.44)
508	Hurst Park, Surrey		Domestic accomm. for LSs
403	Kingston Bagpuize, Oxon		4th TAD and associated
			ADGs, SGs and MR&RSs
—	Kingston Deverill, Wilts.		Domestic accomm. for LSs
—	Knook Camp, Wilts.		40th Mobile Comms. Sqdn. (dets. ZQ and ZU)
			21st Weather Sqdn. (dets. ZQ and ZU)
—	Knutsford, Cheshire		Domestic accomm. for LSs
460	Marks Hall, Essex	IX BC	HQ IX BC (11.43—9.44)
—	Marlborough, Wilts.		40th Mobile Comms. Sqdn. (det. YD)
			21st Weather Sqdn. (det. YD)
166	Matching, Essex	IX AFSC	13th RCD (11.43—6.44)
466	Membury, Wilts.	IX AFSC	6th TAD and associated
			ADGs, SGs and MR&RSs
—	Nantwich (Camp Doddington), Cheshire		Domestic accomm. for LSs
—	Northwich, Cheshire		40th Mobile Comms. Sqdn. (det. YC)
			21st Weather Sqdn. (det. YC)
479	North Witham, Lincs.	IX AFSC	1st TAD and associated
			ADGs, SGs and MR&RSs
—	Plymouth, Devon		1st Air Combat Control Sqdn. (Amphibious)

451	Rudloe Manor, Wilts.	IX TAC	HQ IX TAC
361	Snailwell, Cambs.	IX AFSC	Aircraft Assembly Depot and associated MR&RSs
424	Sole Common, ?	IX EC	EABs
169	Stansted, Essex	IX AFSC	2nd TAD and associated ADGs, SGs and MR&RSs
442	Totton, Hants.		13th RCD
537	Trowbridge, Wilts.		Activation point for some MR&RSs
409	Uxbridge, Middlesex		HQ IX ASC/TAC (2.44—6.44)
—	Weston-super-Mare, Somerset		40th Mobile Comms. Sqdn. (det. YF)
			21st Weather Sqdn. (det. YF)
450	Zeals, Wilts.		5th TAD and associated ADGs, SGs and MR&RSs (1.44—3.44)

APPENDIX D: ORDERS OF BATTLE

ORDER OF BATTLE 9.6.44

IX BOMBER COMMAND

97th Combat Wing (Light)

409th Bomb Group	Little Walden	A-20
410th Bomb Group	Gosfield	A-20
416th Bomb Group	Wethersfield	A-20

98th Combat Wing (Medium)

323rd Bomb Group	Earls Colne	B-26
387th Bomb Group	Chipping Ongar	B-26
394th Bomb Group	Boreham	B-26
397th Bomb Group	Rivenhall	B-26

99th Combat Wing (Medium)

322nd Bomb Group	Andrews Field	B-26
344th Bomb Group	Stansted	B-26
386th Bomb Group	Great Dunmow	B-26
391st Bomb Group	Matching	B-26

IX TACTICAL AIR COMMAND

70th Fighter Wing

48th Fighter Group	Ibsley	P-47
367th Fighter Group	Stoney Cross	P-38
371st Fighter Group	Bisterne	P-47
474th Fighter Group	Warmwell	P-38

71st Fighter Wing

366th Fighter Group	Thruxton	P-47
368th Fighter Group	Chilbolton	P-47
370th Fighter Group	Andover	P-38

84th Fighter Wing

50th Fighter Group	Lymington	P-47
365th Fighter Group	Beaulieu	P-47
404th Fighter Group	Winkton	P-47
405th Fighter Group	Christchurch	P-47
67th Tactical Reconnaissance Group	Middle Wallop etc.	(various)

XIX TACTICAL AIR COMMAND

100th Fighter Wing

354th Fighter Group	Lashenden	P-51
358th Fighter Group	High Halden	P-47
362nd Fighter Group	Headcorn	P-47
363rd Fighter Group	Staplehurst	P-51

303rd Fighter Wing

36th Fighter Group	Kingsnorth	P-47
373rd Fighter Group	Woodchurch	P-47
406th Fighter Group	Ashford	P-47

IX TROOP CARRIER COMMAND

50th Troop Carrier Wing		
439th Troop Carrier Group	Upottery	C-47, C-53
440th Troop Carrier Group	Exeter	C-47, CG-4
441st Troop Carrier Group	Merryfield	C-47, C-53, CG-4
442nd Troop Carrier Group	Weston Zoyland	C-47, C-53, CG-4
52nd Troop Carrier Wing		
61st Troop Carrier Group	Barkston Heath	C-47, CG-4
313rd Troop Carrier Group	Folkingham	C-47, C-53, CG-4
314th Troop Carrier Group	Saltby	C-47, C-53, CG-4
315th Troop Carrier Group	Spanhoe	C-47, C-53, CG-4
316th Troop Carrier Group	Cottesmore	C-47, C-53, CG-4
53rd Troop Carrier Wing		
434th Troop Carrier Group	Aldermaston	C-47, C-53, CG-4
435th Troop Carrier Wing	Welford	C-47, C-53, CG-4
436th Troop Carrier Group	Membury	C-47, CG-4
437th Troop Carrier Group	Ramsbury	C-47, C-53, CG-4
438th Troop Carrier Group	Greenham Common	C-47, C-53, CG-4

IX AIR FORCE SERVICE COMMAND

1st Advanced Air Depot Area		
1 Tactical Air Depot	North Witham	
2 Tactical Air Depot	Stansted	
3 Tactical Air Depot	Grove	
2nd Advanced Air Depot Area		
4 Tactical Air Depot	Kingston Bagpuize	
5 Tactical Air Depot	Chilbolton	
6 Tactical Air Depot	Membury	
Transport Wing		
31st Air Transport Group	Grove	(various)

LIAISON SQUADRONS

14th Liaison Squadron	Cranage/Knutsford*	L-5, UC-78
47th Liaison Squadron	Heston	L-5, UC-78
112th Liaison Squadron	Kingston Deverill*	nil
125th Liaison Squadron	Cheltenham*	nil
153rd Liaison Squadron	New Zealand Farm/Erle Stoke*	L-5

OTHER UNITS

10th Photographic Recon. Group	Chalgrove	(various)
1st Pathfinder Squadron	Andrews Field	B-26
422nd Nightfighter Squadron	Scorton	P-61
425th Nightfighter Squadron	Charmy Down	nil
3rd CCRC	Toome	A-20, B-26
IX TCC Pathfinder School	North Witham	C-47, C-53

*domestic accommodation

One of the hacks used by the 391st BG while at Matching was this UC-61A, 14605
[R. Mynn]

IX AIR FORCE SERVICE COMMAND

1st Transport Group (Prov.)	Creil	(various)
31st Air Transport Group	Grove	(various)

9th AIR DIVISION

Combat Wing (Medium)

323rd Bomb Group	Denain/Prouvy	B-26
387th Bomb Group	Maastricht/Beek	B-26
394th Bomb Group	Venlo	B-26
397th Bomb Group	Venlo	A-26

Combat Wing (Medium)

322nd Bomb Group	Fritzlar (HQ)	B-26
344th Bomb Group	Florennes/Juzaines	B-26
386th Bomb Group	St. Trond	A-26
391st Bomb Group	Asch	A-26

Combat Wing (Light)

409th Bomb Group	Laon/Couvron	A-20
410th Bomb Group	Juvincourt	A-20
416th Bomb Group	Laon/Athies	A-20

IX TACTICAL AIR COMMAND

70th Fighter Wing

36th Fighter Group	Kassel/Rothwesten	P-47
365th Fighter Group	Fritzlar	P-47
404th Fighter Group	Fritzlar	P-47
474th Fighter Group	Langensalza	P-38
67th Tactical Recon. Group	Eschwege	(various)
422nd Night Fighter Squadron	Langensalza	P-61

XIX TACTICAL AIR COMMAND

100th Fighter Wing

48th Fighter Group	lllesheim	P-47
354th Fighter Group	Ansbach	P-51
362nd Fighter Group	lllesheim	P-47
367th Fighter Group	Frankfurt/Eschborn	P-47
368th Fighter Group	Frankfurt-am-Main	P-47
371st Fighter Group	Furth	P-47
405th Fighter Group	Straubing	P-47
10th Photo Recon. Group	Furth	(various)
425th Night Fighter Squadron	Furth	P-61
14th Liaison Squadron	Regensburg	L-5

XIX TACTICAL AIR COMMAND

84th and 303rd Fighter Wings

366th Fighter Group	Munster/Handorf	P-47
370th Fighter Group	Gutersloh	P-51
373rd Fighter Group	Lippstadt	P-47
406th Fighter Group	Munster/Handorf	P-47
363rd Tactical Recon. Group	Braunschweig	P-38, P-51, F-3, F-5, F-6, A-26
125th Liaison Squadron	Braunshweig	L-5

LIAISON SQUADRONS

47th Liaison Squadron	Wiesbaden	L-5
72nd Liaison Squadron	Augsburg	L-5
112th Liaison Squadron	Buc	L-5
153rd Liaison Squadron	Weimar	L-5
158th Liaison Squadron	Ahrweiler	L-5
167th Liaison Squadron	Pfaffengrund	L-5
173rd Liaison Squadron	Paris/Orly	L-5

OTHER UNITS

516th Troop Carrier Group	?	
IX TCC Pathfinder Group	Chartres	C-47, C-53, C-109

APPENDIX E: THE MOBILE REPAIR AND RECLAMATION SQUADRONS

Brief details of the Mobile Reclamation & Repair Squadrons' bases and tasks are given below:

Base	Date	Tasks
21st MR&RS		
Matching	6.11.43	Activation
Filton	24.11.43	Assembly of P-47s, P-51s and A-20s
Chilbolton	20.6.44	Dets. to ALGs (Note 1)
Kingston Bagpuize	31.7.44	Dets. to ALGs (Note 2)
Stansted	29.8.44	Repairs to B-26s (Note 3)
Grove	10.10.44	Assembly of L-4s and L-5s, for FA
Cambrai (F)	3.11.44	B-26 salvage
Liege/Bierset (B)	12.5.45	Fitting ferry tanks to A-26s
Kassel/Waldau (G)	5.7.45 — 12.45	Storage of B-24s and gliders
22nd MR&RS		
Matching	5.11.43	Activation
Ramsbury	22.11.43	In transit
Filton	25.11.43	Assembly of P-47, P-51, A-20 P-38, AT-6 and UC-64 aircraft
Membury	18.6.44	Dets. to Lashenden
Lashenden	11.7.44	P-51 salvage
Membury	19.7.44	Training
Reims (F)	15.9.44	Dets. to Villacoublay etc.
Liege (B)	22.10.44	B-17s and C-47s
Hanau (G)	5.45	
Leipheim (G)	29.10.45	Inactivation
23rd MR&RS		
Matching	1.11.43	Activation
Grove	16.11.43	Assembly of L-4s and L-5s for FA
Cricqueville (F)	18.6.44	L-4 and L-5 battle damage
St. Gilles (F)	1.8.44	ditto
Barenton (F)	17.8.44	ditto
Epernon (F)	28.8.44	ditto
Guise (F)	8.9.44	ditto
St. Georges (B)	14.9.44	ditto
Theux (B)	2.11.44	ditto
St. Georges (B)	18.12.44	ditto
Stockay (B)	21.12.44	ditto
Fexhe-le-Haut-Clocker (B)	26.12.44	ditto
Cuchenheim (G)	14.3.45	ditto
Ehringhausen (G)	4.4.45	ditto
Hofgeismar (G)	12.4.45	ditto
Jena (G)	30.4.45	ditto
Rotogen (G)	19.5.45	ditto
Holzkirchen (G)	11.6.45	Storeage of 400 B-17s
Clastres (F)	17.7.45	Inactivation
24th MR&RS		
Grove	1.11.43	Activation
Stansted	21.11.43	In transit
Membury	28.12.43	
Warmwell	25.2.44	(Note 4)
Carentan (F)	26.6.44	Worked with 50th FG; det at Picqueville
Meautis (F)	16.8.44	
Paris/Orly	10.9.44	
Couvron (F)	12.9.44	
Lyons/Bron	23.9.44	
Toul (F)	31.10.44	Det. at Sandhofen (G)
Giebelstadt (G)	24.4.45	
Sandhofen (G)	25.4.45	

Assembling the forward fuselage of a CG-4A at Crookham Common, the vast Glider Assembly Depot in Berkshire
[via D. Benfield]

Clastres (F)	17.7.45	
Luxemburg (L)	?	
Erlangen (G)	14.8.45 — 5.12.45	Salvage
25th MR&RS		
Grove	1.11.43	Activation
Stansted	21.11.43	B-26 maintenance and battle damage
Folkingham	21.2.44	C-47 maintenance
Boreham	2.3.44	B-26 maintenance and battle damage
Gosfield	13.3.44	ditto
Rivenhall	15.4.44	ditto
Christchurch	5.8.44	
Gorges (F)	25.8.44	B-26 salvage and repair
Dreux (F)	12.9.44	ditto
Peronne (F)	6.10.44	ditto
Cambrai (F)	2.11.44	ditto
Venlo (H)	2.5.45	ditto
Tirlemont (B)	30.5.45	ditto
Liege/Bierset (B)	11.6.45 — N/K	Inactivation
26th MR&RS		
Crookham Common	10.11.43 — 30.4.45	Large-scale assembly of gliders
27th MR&RS		
Matching	23.11.43	Activation
Langar	29.11.43	C-47 maintenance
Welford	9.2.44	ditto
North Witham	3.4.44	ditto
Membury	28.6.44	ditto
Le Molay (F)	15.7.44	A-20 and B-26 salvage and repair
Reims (F)	8.10.44	Fighter repair
Neuss/Greenwood strip	6.4.45	L-4 and L-5 salvage and repair
Ansbach (G)	10.7.45	Inactivation
28th MR&RS		
Matching	1.11.43	Activation
Gosfield	29.11.43	B-26 salvage and repair (Note 5)

Andrews Field	27.12.43	B-26 salvage and repair
Beauvais (F)	22.9.44	ditto (Note 6)
Le Culot (B)	7.4.45	ditto
Munchen-Gladbach (G)	29.5.45	Inactivation

29th MR&RS

Camp Griffiss	1.11.43	Activation
Matching	12.11.43	ditto
Gosfield	29.11.43	(Note 7)
Greenham Common (HQ and Det. B)	26.12.43	
Cardonville (F) (Det.A)	18.6.44	
Azeville (F) (HQ and Det. B)	3.7.44	
Chartres (F)	30.8.44	
Laon/Athies(F)	13.9.44	
Chievres (B)	7.10.44	
Metz (F)	12.1.45	
Florennes/Juzaines (B)	?	
Weides (G)	23.3.45	
Fritzlar (G)	15.4.45	
Kassel (G)	6.6.45	
Liege (B)	7.6.45	Inactivation

30th MR&RS

Matching	23.11.43	Activation
Fulbeck	29.11.43	
Charmy Down	29.12.43	
Kingston Bagpuize	7.2.44	
Charmy Down	12.3.44	
Ashford	4.4.44	Worked with 406th FG (Note 23)
Tour-en-Bessin (F)	24.7.44	
Maupertus (F)	16.8.44	Detached to Vannes to work on P-61s
Chateaudun (F)	30.8.44	
Florennes (B)	28.9.44	Worked on 422nd NFS P-61s
Coulommiers (F)	29.9.44	
Reims (F)	13.10.44	
Etain (F)	10.11.44	
Reims/Champagne (F)	15.3.45	
Ansbach (G)	17.5.45	
Bremen (G)	7.7.45	Clearance of buildings for IDG
Eschwege (G)	21.9.45 — 12.45	Storeage of 400 P-47s

31st MR&RS

Matching	1.11.43	Activation
Hitcham	27.11.43	Various tasks on 8th AF aircraft
Membury	25.1.44	7th ADG
Holmsley South	24.2.44	(Note 8)
Omelmont (F)	?	(Note 9)
Luneville (F)	28.3.45 — 8.45	Inactivation

32nd MR&RS

Matching	23.11.43	Activation
Wattisham	30.11.43	
Zeals	5.12.43	Setting up 5th TAD
Chilbolton	8.1.44	Training
Warmwell	24.2.44	ditto
Ibsley	1.3.44	ditto
Stoney Cross	15.3.44	ditto
Ibsley	6.7.44	ditto
St. Marie du Mont (F)	30.7.44	Maintenance of P-38s of 367th FG
Brucheville (F)	2.8.44	ditto
Cricqueville (F)	13.8.44	ditto
St. Jean de Daye (F)	20.8.44	ditto
Peray (F)	6.9.44	
Clastres (F)	14.9.44	
Juvincourt (F)	25.10.44	
St. Dizier (F)	7.2.44	
Conflans (F)	16.3.44	
Eschborn (G)	14.4.44	
Kassel (G)	5.44	
Munchen-Gladbach (G)	23.5.44	Inactivation

33rd MR&RS

Camp Griffiss	1.11.43	Activation
Matching	12.11.43	ditto
Filton	4.12.43	Aircraft assembly
Snailwell	21.5.44	Aircraft Replacement Centre (Notes 10 and 11)

Grove	24.7.44	
Crookham Common	9.8.44	Glider Assembly Depot (Note 12)
Orleans (F)	1.1.45	P-47 and C-47 salvage; preparation of CG-4s

34th MR&RS
Dealt with motor transport only

35th MR&RS

Matching	14.11.43	Activation
Membury	24.11.43	Training (Note 13)
Thruxton	28.2.44	
St. Pierre du Mont (F)	7.44	
Dreux (F)	28.8.44	
Laon/Couvron (F)	9.9.44	
Asch (B)	7.11.44	
Handorf (G)	16.4.45	
Kassel (G)	24.4.45	
Munchen-Gladbach (G)	30.5.45	Inactivation

36th MR&RS

Matching	1.11.43	Activation
Keevil	21.11.43	
Chilbolton	24.1.44	
Raydon	26.2.44	(Note 14)
High Halden	8.4.44	
Staplehurst	13.4.44	
Maupertus (F)	2.7.44	Worked with 358th and 363rd FGs
Cretteville (F)	?	
Pontorson (F)	18.8.44	
Mourmelon-le-Grande (F)	?	
St. Dizier (F)	11.44	P-51 maintenance (Note 15)
Ophoven (B)	5.2.45	Worked with 405th FG
Kitzingen (G)	?	
Straubing (G)	10.5.45	
Creil (F)	15.6.45	Storeage of 750 fighters B-26s and L-5s

37th MR&RS
No record

38th MR&RS
No record

39th MR&RS

Matching	14.11.43	Activation
Earls Colne	1.1.44	(Note 16)
Beaulieu	18.7.44	
Lessay (F)	22.8.44	
Chartres (F)	18.9.44	(Note 17)
Cambrai ( )	9.10.44	
Denain (F)	?	
Oberweisenfeld (G)	19.5.45	Maintenance of 387th BG aircraft Inactivated 15.6.45

40th MR&RS

Matching	15.11.43	Activation
Chipping Ongar	22.11.43	(Note 18)
Matching	27.12.43	Repairs to B-26s and P-47s
Roye/Amy (F)	26.9.44	
Beauvais/Tille	18.10.44	
Roye/Amy (F)	20.2.45	(Note 20)
Asch (B)	20.4.45	
R-94 (?)	?	Glider storage (inactivated 31.12.43)

41st MR&RS

Matching	5.12.43	Activation
Wattisham (8th AF)	1.1.44	
Mendlesham (8th AF)	7.1.44	
Langar	15.3.44	
Stansted	24.4.44	Servicing B-26s
Snailwell	7.5.44	Operated reserve pool of aircraft
Grove	22.5.44	Attached to 31st ATG to 20.7.44
Stansted	9.9.44	Fully mobile squadron
Grove	8.10.44	Assembly of L-4s and L-5s (Note 21)
Melun/Villaroche (F)	25.10.44	Fully mobile squadron
Laon/Couvron (F)	17.2.45	Crated equipment for PTO
Ansbach (G)	7.45	Repairs to aircraft of 326th Ferrying Sqdn.; inactivated 31.12.45

42nd MR&RS

Trowbridge	5.12.43	Activation
Filton	3.1.44	
Boreham	22.1.44	
Langar	2.3.44	
Folkingham	11.3.44	(Note 22)
Grove	21.4.44	Attached to 31st ATG
Creil (F)	23.9.44	Initially attached to 1st ATG (Prov.)
Ansbach (G)	22.5.45	Attached to 1st ATG (Prov.)
		Inactivated 30.10.45

43rd MR&RS

Trowbridge	5.12.43	Activation
Zeals	4.1.44	
Chilbolton	8.1.44	
Balderton	18.2.44	Laid temporary runway
Grove	5.4.44	Assembled L-4 and L-5 aircraft
Nehou (F)	10.7.44	Maintenance of L-4s and L-5s for US Third Army
Cavray (F)	6.8.44	ditto
La Bezoge (F)	16.8.44	ditto
Brou (F)	21.8.44	ditto
Courcy-aux-Loges (F)	28.8.44	ditto
Marson (F)	7.9.44	ditto
Braquis (F)	13.9.44	ditto
Riaville (F)	16.10.44	ditto
Bettelainville (F)	30.11.44	ditto
Bad Kreuznach (C)	24.3.45	ditto
Ziegenhain (G)	3.4.45	ditto

Mud, packing cases and Waco CG-4A gliders in various stages of assembly; an aerial view of the Glider Assembly Depot, Crookham Common
[via D. Benfield]

Eisenbach (G)	10.4.45	ditto
Herzogenaurach (G)	20.4.45	ditto
Ergolding (G)	5.5.45	
Vilseck (G)	28.5.45	
Leipheim	28.10.45	For inactivation on 30.10.45

44th MR&RS

Matching	5.12.43	Activation
Trowbridge	24.12.43	
Cottesmore	4.1.44	
North Witham	27.1.44	
Langar	27.5.44	Modification and repair of 350 CG-4 gliders
Chilbolton	24.6.44	
Bishopstrow	2.7.44	
Le Molay (F)	20.7.44	Repair and reclamation in the field
Le Mans	21.8.44	
Villacoublay (F)	30.8.44	
Asch (B)	2.3.45	
Kelz (G)	12.4.45	
Fritzlar (G)	16.4.45	From VE- Day located and handled captured aircraft for 5th Air Disarmament Group
Nordholz (G)	4.6.45	Serviced L-4s and L-5s of US Seventh Army
Goppingen (G)	1.8.45	Inactivated 31.12.45

45th MR&RS

Trowbridge	5.12.43	Activation
Filton	3.1.44	
Zeals	22.1.44	
Woodchurch	10.3.44	
Kingsnorth	16.3.44	Serviced fighters on line
St. Marie du Mont (F)	12.7.44	
Tour-en-Bessin	1.8.44	Serviced fighters
St. James (F)	25.8.44	ditto
Athis (F)	?	ditto
Juvincourt (F)	8.10.44	ditto
Le Culot (B)	27.10.44	
Kassel/Rothwesten (G)	?	
Ansbach (G)	25.6.45	Serviced L-4s and L-5s for US Third Army; final fate unknown

46th MR&RS

Stansted	5.12.43	
Wethersfield	17.2.44	
Little Walden	23.2.44	
Melun/Villaroche (F)	9.44	
Laon/Athies (F)	20.2.45	
Le Culot (B)	16.5.45	
Clastres (F)	16.6.45 — N/K	

47th MR&RS

Trowbridge	31.12.43	Activation
Fulbeck	4.1.44	C-47 maintenance
Aldermaston	9.3.44	ditto
Stansted	11.5.44	B-26 maintenance
Beauvais/Tille (F)	14.10.44	ditto, including Free French aircraft
Le Culot (B)	9.4.45	Preparing Luftwaffe aircraft for shipment to USA
Illesheim (G)	7.9.45	B-26 and A- 26 salvage; inactivated 5.12.45

48th MR&RS

?	5.12.43	Activation
Aldermaston	2.44	
Florennes/Juzaines (B)	?	
Ophoven (B)	28.1.45	
Gutersloh (G)	?	
Le Culot (B)	31.5.45	
Clastres (F)	13.6.45 — N/K	

49th MR&RS

?	5.12.43	Activation
Chalgrove	?	
Rennes (F)	9.8.44	

Chateaudun (F)	29.8.44	
St. Dizier (F)	9.9.44	Servicing A-20s of 155th PRS
Conflans (F)	24.11.44	P-51 modifications
Trier/Evren (G)	27.3.45	
Ober Olm (G)	2.4.45	
Furth (G)	?	
Cambrai (F)	29.5.45	Preparing A-26s for PTO
Goppingen (G)	21.9.45	Storage of L-4s; inactivated 31.12.45
50th MR&RS		
?	20.12.43	Activation
Crookham Common	17.1.44	Glider assembly
Grove	10.7.44	Assembly of L-4s and L-5s
Rennes/St. Jacques (F)	14.9.44	Servicing and repair of L-4s of the FA
Maastricht (H)	21.10.44	ditto
Munchen Gladbach (G)	12.3.45	
Bielefeld (G)	18.4.45	
Hessich/Lichtenau (G)	29.6.45	
Eschwege (G)	29.9.45	Inactivated 30.10.45

Notes.

1. ALGs at Lymington, Bisterne, Ibsley, Beaulieu, Winkton and Christchurch were visited.
2. ALGs at Kingsnorth and Woodchurch and airfields at Middle Wallop, Warmwell, Andover and Membury (to service UC-64s and UC-78s) were visited.
3. Teams were sent to Hurn, Beaulieu, Matching, Andrews Field, Stoney Cross and Holmsley South to repair B-26s; two teams to Scorton to service P-61s; and teams to Little Walden, Wethersfield and Gosfield to repair A-20s.
4. The squadron split into two on 1.3.44; Det. 'A' went to Christchurch to work with 405th FG and Det. 'B' to Lymington to work with 50th FG.
5. Detachment at Stansted.
6. Detachment at Cormeilles-en-Vexin.
7. Det. 'A' was formed at Gosfield to work with 365th FG; to Beaulieu 12.3.44.
8. Detachment to Bisterne to work on P-47s.
9. Det. 'A' serviced P-47s of 371st FG at Tantonville; Det. 'B' serviced P-51s and P-38s of XII TAC at Azelot; Det. 'C' serviced P-47s of 324th FG at Luneville.
10. Prepared up to 100 A-20s for service.
11. Detachments at Langar and Bottesford in 6.44 to inspect and rectify gliders.
12. Detachments sent to Langar, Methwold, Biggin Hill, Fulbeck, Aldermaston, North Witham, Boreham, Greenham Common and Balderton at this time.
13. Detachment at Middle Wallop to assist 67th TRG.
14. Detachment at Rivenhall at end of 2.44 to work on B-26s.
15. P-51s of 8th Air Force's 361st FG on detachment.
16. Detachment at Great Dunmow
17. Detachments at Beaumont-sur-Oise, Chateaudun, St. Quentin and Laon.
18. Detachment at Stoney Cross.
19. Detachments at Maupertus from 23.8.44 and at Lombron from 19.9.44.
20. Detachments at Beaumont-sur-Oise from 15.10.44 and at St. Trond from 10.4.45.
21. Detachment at Fulbeck from 3.3.44.
22. Detachment at Greenham Common.
23. Detached to Scorton 25.5.44 to work on P-61s.

APPENDIX F:
THE ENGINEER AVIATION REGIMENTS AND BATTALIONS

Brief details of the Engineer Aviation Brigades, Regiments and Battalions are given below:

Brigades:

1st Engineer Aviation Brigade:

Activated 1.8.44 as a means of decentralising control; worked in close proximity to TAC and Army which it supported.

2nd Engineer Aviation Brigade:

as 1st EAB

3rd Engineer Aviation Brigade:

Activated winter 1944/45

Regiments:

922nd Engineer Aviation Regiment:

(no details available)

923rd Engineer Aviation Regiment:

Arrived in France 9.44; employed on airfields on the southern front in support of French 1st Army and US 7th Army.

924th Engineer Aviation Regiment:

Arrived in UK 7.43; built 28 airstrips in England in 12 months; to France on D + 32; built or rebuilt 47 airfields on the Continent; after the Rhine crossing detachments moved with infantry to repair S&E airfields for rapid use.

925th Engineer Aviaition Regiment:

Sometime based at Great Barrington in England; arrived at Omaha Beach on 2.7.44; built 77 airstrips in ten months; followed the army east via Paris to winter in the Metz area, then pushed into Germany, ending at Munich.

926th Engineer Aviation Regiment:

Originally based at Honington with the 8th Air Force, for which it carried out 28 jobs; then moved to Great Barrington, with practice moves to Wethersfield and Cokethorpe; landed in France on D + 5; followed the Army from Cherbourg to Pilsen in Czechoslovakia; built 76 airfields.

Battalions:

816th Engineer Aviation Battalion:

Was in the UK for 18 months building 8th Air Force bases; transferred to 9th Air Force; operated in France from D + 8; built airstrip A-3, Cardonville; advanced through France into Germany, where it built eight S&E airstrips in three days.

818th Engineer Aviation Battalion:

Arrived on Utah Beach on 30.6.44; followed the advance through France to Luxemburg and Nancy; built 18 airfields in France and twelve S&E strips east of the Rhine.

819th Engineer Aviation Battalion:

Built Andrews Field for the 8th Air Force before transferring to the 9th; elements landed in Normandy on D-Day; built ten ALGs and 14 S&E air-strips; rebuilt three enemy airfields.

820th Engineer Aviation Battalion:

Was employed for two years on airfield construction in England; arrived on Omaha Beach on D + 1; followed the advance into Belgium and across the Rhine.

825th Engineer Aviation Battalion:

(no details available)

826th Engineer Aviation Battalion:

Arrived in Normandy on D + 6; Built A-10, Carentan, in six days while under artillery fire; built airfields behind the US 7th and 9th Armies; had moved deep into Germany by VE-Day.

830th Engineer Aviation Battalion:

Spent 22 months working for the 8th Air Force before joining the 9th; moved to Normandy and built 13 airfields.

832nd Engineer Aviation Battalion:

Built Glatton airfield and Abotts Ripton Depot for the 8th Air Force before moving to the 9th's ALGs in Kent, which it then maintained; arrived in France on D + 24; built ten airfields and 16 S&E airstrips and maintained nine others.

833rd Engineer Aviation Battalion:

Worked for the 8th Air Force before transferring to the 9th; arrived at Omaha Beach on 30.6.44; no further information.

834th Engineer Aviation Battalion:

Constructed Matching airfield for 8th AF; assigned to 9th AF 12.43; carried out training at Chisledon, Torquay, Matching and Great Barrington; landed Omaha Beach on D-Day; built ELS at St. Laurent-sur-Mer (first C-47 landed early 9.6.44); constructed St. Pierre du Mont, Le Molay, Courtils, Lombron; refurbished St. Trond (Belgium) and various airfields in France; Built Niedermendig, Ailertchen and Limburg in Germany and Pilsen in Czechoslovakia and rebuilt Erfurt.

837th Engineer Aviation Battalion:

Saw service in Africa, Italy and the MTO before joining IX EC in 3.45; worked at Marseilles.

840th Engineer Aviation Battalion:

Arrived in Normandy early 7.44; advanced with the Army through France to Stuttgart.

843rd Engineer Aviation Battalion:

Arrived in Normandy on D+25; Built 40 airfields; was in Munich on VE-Day.

846th Engineer Aviation Battalion:

Arrived in Normandy on 16.7.44; completed airstrip A-13 (Tour-en-Bessin) in ten days; then moved through France to end at Bremen.

847th Engineer Aviation Battalion:

Was with 1st TAF until 2.45; built medium-bomber airfields at Lyon and Dijon.

850th Engineer Aviation Battalion:

Arrived on Utah Beach on D+14; advanced through France and into Germany.

851st Engineer Aviation Battalion:

Maintained seven ALGs in SE England before moving to France and on into Germany.

852nd Engineer Aviation Battalion:

Arrived in UK 5.43; moved to Normandy on D+37; then advanced through France and into Germany.

859th Engineer Aviation Battalion:

Built an 8th Air Force airfield before moving to France; finally into Germany.

861st Engineer Aviation Battalion:

Arrived in UK 5.43; built Boreham airfield; then employed on maintenance of 8th Air Force bases.

862nd Engineer Aviation Battalion:

Was in the UK for 14 months (at Birch from 26.4.44); then moved through France into Belgium; at one time maintained all USAAF airfields in Belgium and Holland.

876th Airborne Engineer Aviation Battalion:

Was at Sole Common, Berkshire, by 7.43 and became the first unit assigned to IX EC; carried out mainly maintenance on airfields in France, Belgium and Germany.

877th Airborne Engineer Aviation Battalion:

Arrived in the UK (Bruern Abbey) in 3.44; moved to Normandy on D+30; built A-15, Maupertus, the first B-26 airfield on the Continent; was involved in the construction or maintenance of 66 airfields on the Continent.

878th Airborne Engineer Aviation Battalion:

Arrived in the UK (Sole Common, Berkshire) in 3.44; apparently did not see any active service until it was involved in Operation Market Garden at Armhem.

The 861st EAB boasted a dance band, The Castle Airs, seen here at Boreham providing music to enthusiastic dancers
[Bryan Jones]

APPENDIX G: 9th AIR FORCE GROUP AND SQUADRON CODE LETTERS

Code	Squadron	Group
AJ	356th FS	354th FG
AN	553rd BS	386th BG
AX	107th TRS	67th TRG
CH	365th FS	358th FG
CJ	71st TCS	434th TCG
CM	78th TCS	435th TCG
CN	73rd TCS	434th TCG
CP	367th FS	358th FG
CU	72nd TCS	434th TCG
CW	76th TCS	435th TCG
DR	452nd BS	322nd BG
ER	450th BS	322nd BG
FT	353rd FS	354th FG
FW	556th BS	387th BG
GQ	355th FS	354th FG
IA	366th FS	358th FG
IB	77th TCS	435th TCG
ID	74th TCS	434th TCG
IH	1st PFS	(TCC)
KS	557th BS	387th BG
KX	558th BS	387th BG
NM	34th TCS	315th TCG
PN	449th BS	322nd BG
QL	22nd TRS	69th TRG
RG	552nd BS	386th BG
RJ	454th BS	323rd BG
RU	554th BS	386th BG
SH	75th TCS	435th TCG
SS	451st BS	322nd BG
SW	33rd PRS	10th PG/67th TRG
TQ	559th BS	387th BG
UA	43rd TCS	315th TCG
VT	453rd BS	323rd BG
VX	109th TRS	69th TRG
WT	456th BS	323rd BG
XX	34th PS	69th TRG
YA	555th BS	386th BG
YC	10th TRS	69th TRG
YU	455th BS	323rd BG
ZM	12th TRS	67th TRG/10th PRG
ZS	12th TRS	67th TRG
A6	389th FS	366th FG
A7	395th FS	368th FG
A8	391st FS	366th FG
A9	380th FS	363rd FG
	160th TRS	363rd TRG
B2	390th FS	366th FG
B3	381st FS	363rd FG
	161st TRS	363rd TRG
B4	387th FS	365th FG
B6	363rd FS	357th FG
B8	379th FS	362nd FG
C2	396th FS	368th FG
C3	382nd FS	363rd FG
	162nd TRS	363rd TRG
C4	388th FS	365th FG
C5	364th FS	357th FG
D3	397th FS	368th FG
D5	386th FS	365th FG
D6	642nd BS	409th BG
D8	94th TCS	439th TCG
E4	377th FS	362nd FG
E5	62nd TCS	314th TCG
E6	402nd FS	370th FG
F4	492nd FS	48th FG
F5	428th FS	474th FG
F6	670th BS	416th BG
G4	362nd FS	357th FG
G8	378th FS	362nd FG
G9	509th FS	405th FG
H2	49th TCS	313rd TCG
H5	392nd FS	367th FG
H9	586th BS	394th BG
I6	30th PS	10th PG
I7	493rd FS	48th FG
J7	303rd TCS	442nd TCG
J8	92nd TCS	439th TCG
K4	511th FS	405th FG
K5	584th BS	394th BG
K6	430th FS	474th FG
K9	494th BS	344th BG
L3	512th FS	406th FG
L4	91st TCS	439th TCG
M2	88th TCS	438th TCG
M6	309th TCS	315th TCG
N3	47th TCS	313rd TCG
	496th BS	344th BG
N5	111th TRS	69th TRG
O7	514th FS	406th FG
O8	575th BS	391st BG
P2	572nd BS	391st BG
Q7	90th TCS	438th TCG
Q8	23rd TCS	349th TCG
Q9	61st TCS	314th TCG
R3	410th FS	373rd FG
S2	32nd TCS	314th TCG
S6	79th TCS	436th TCG
S9	34th PS	10th PG
T2	83rd TCS	437th TCG
T3	45th TCS	316th TCG
T5	10th FS	50th FG
T6	573rd BS	391st BG
U2	598th BS	397th BG
U5	81st TCS	436th TCG
U9	411th FS	373rd FG
V4	304th TCS	442nd TCG
V5	412th FS	373rd FG
W3	313th FS	50th FG
W5	640th BS	409th BG
W6	97th TCS	440th TCG
W7	37th TCS	316th TCG
X2	596th BS	397th BG
X5	59th TCS	61st TCG
Y5	495th BS	344th BG
Y8	507th FS	404th FG
Y9	15th TCS	61st TCG
Z4	301st TCS	441st TCG
Z7	48th TCS	313rd TCG
Z8	84th TCS	437th TCG
2A	669th BS	416th BG
2L	302nd TCS	441st TCG
2N	81st FS	50th FG
2R	50th TCS	314th TCG
2W	33rd PS	363rd TRG
2Z	510th FS	405th FG
3A	53rd TCS	61st TCG
3B	93rd TCS	439th TCG
3D	82nd TCS	436th TCG
3F	313th TCS	349th TCG
3I	14th TCS	61st TCG
3J	99th TCS	441st TCG
3T	22nd FS	36th FG
3X	87th TCS	438th TCG
4A	310th TCS	315th TCG
4C	44th TCS	316th TCG
4J	305th TCS	442nd TCG
4K	506th FS	404th FG
4L	574th BS	391st BG
4N	394th FS	367th FG
4P	513th FS	406th FG
4T	585th BS	394th BG
4U	89th TCS	438th TCG
4W	406th FS	371st FG
5C	671st BS	416th BG
5D	644th BS	410th BG
5H	668th BS	416th BG
5I	643rd BS	409th BG
5K	86th TCS	437th TCG
5M	15th TRS	10th PG/67th TRG
5X	29th TCS	313th TCG
5W	587th BS	394th BG
6B	599th BS	397th BG
6C	14th LS	
6E	36th TCS	316th TCG
6M	494th FS	48th FG
6Q	647th BS	410th BG
6V	53rd FS	36th FG
6Z	96th TCS	440th TCG
7D	80th TCS	436th TCG
7F	485th FS	370th FG
7G	641st BS	409th BG
7H	306th TCS	442nd TCG
7I	497th BS	344th BG
7J	508th FS	404th FG
7U	23rd FS	36th FG
7X	645th BS	410th BG
7Y	429th FS	474th FG
8C	100th TCS	441st TCG
8L	393rd FS	367th FG
8N	405th FS	371st FG
8R	153rd LS	
8U	646th BS	410th BG
8V	31st PS	10th PG
8Y	98th TCS	440th TCG
9D	401st FS	370th FG
9E	312th TCS	349th TCG
9F	597th BS	397th BG
9O	85th TCS	437th TCG
9Q	404th FS	371st FG
9S	14th LS	
9X	95th TCS	440th TCG

436th TCG C-47 coded 3D:X above a
cloudscape before D-Day   [Lawrence Riordan]

'Blind Date', another 397th BG B-26 with an appreciable number of
raids to its credit   [B. Stait]